MW01101124

Philosophy of Love

Philosophy of Love

Josef Madlener

VANTAGE PRESS
New York

Published by Vantage Press, Inc.
516 West 34th Street, New York, New York 10001

Manufactured in the United States of America
ISBN: 0-533-11369-5

Library of Congress Catalog Card No.: 94-90814

0 9 8 7 6 5 4 3 2 1

In honor to the Creator,
"God of Love,"
and to all living souls
who seek His will
and live in the
philosophy
*   of   *
love

This book is dedicated to
my beloved wife, Iris,
and our shared
companionship
on this journey
of the living
soul
*

GOD OF LOVE

HIS WILL IS

MANIFESTED IN THE

PHILOSOPHY

OF

LOVE

Contents

Philosophy of Love

Introduction

This book is written to honor the "God of Love" and His Holy Spirit. In my search to find Him, no stone was left unturned. I joined various churches, a mystical organization, and meditation groups. I read the Old and New Testaments and was also influenced by the forceful preaching of TV evangelists. At one time my wife and I also attended a crusade in the early sixties in Calgary. The singing was always appealing in the churches because it lifted my spirit; otherwise, I left with uncertainty and an empty soul. The glitter of the churches and their traditions could not translate to me the love of God, nor was there any satisfying explanation of a relationship between God and man. The only connection made clear was that if you don't love God, you might burn in hell for ever.

Since the whole world believes in a higher Spirit in one way or another, I had this burning desire to find out for myself if there is a God. How does man truly relate to the Spirit of God and His boundaries? Upon reading the New Testament, there were verses in Matthew 7:7–8 that flared like a light in my soul: "Ask and it shall be given you; seek, and ye shall find; knock, and it shall be opened unto you: For everyone that asketh receiveth; and he that seeketh findeth; and to him that knocketh it shall be opened." I decided to attempt to confirm those promises to see if they would come true as Jesus said. That prompted my resolution to find the God of Love. I started praying daily whenever I found the time. Gradually I was asking God all sorts of questions, which I hoped one day would be answered.

This became my hobby and so important that all my spare time was spent in studying various religions and books of the occult. Whenever I had the chance at night, especially during the long winter months when my working days were short, I studied the Bible from the beginning to the end. One day, while I was pondering a question I had put before God, I somehow instantly received the answer. I was amazed because I did not remember reading or hearing it anywhere. Since then inspirations through my soul are frequently received, and today I know those communications are inspirations from the Holy Spirit. My questions are answered, no matter how bizarre and complex, and the reason I know from whence they come is because of the accompanying ecstasy every time it happens.

When we are searching to understand difficult universal principles and laws, they may be given to us in the form of a vision in which we are partakers experiencing the occurrence first-hand so that we will never forget its truth. After one such experience, I felt like walking on air for about three days, and the greatest satisfaction I derive is knowing that this is first-hand knowledge of things man has been wondering about for ages. The passages that we read in the Bible, or in any other old Scriptures, are all hand-me-downs, selected and chosen knowledge from people in the past. If we are sincere seekers, then we will have to verify the truth of man's writings within us from our souls, where the Holy Spirit will enlighten us thereof. At this point I must also mention that any inspiration, dream or vision must be analyzed by the spiritual mixing bowl. However, if you find they clash with any of the virtues of love, then the message is not of the Holy Spirit but of an aberration of the sensual spirit of man.

The God I have found I call the "God of Love" and

bestow upon Him all of creation; any other gods with the characteristics of a duality like man are but part of creation under the heavens. A drop of water cannot, in itself, ever be the sea. How much less of a chance is there for a created living duality to become the mighty over-soul of all creation I call God? This God never had the need to masquerade amongst men in the flesh; those are fantasies distorting the truth, and the worldly spirit of man has been falsely idolized and mistaken for the truth of God. There were many prophets in the past who have interpreted God and His message according to their sensual understanding of the worldly spirit. I am told that any word or action that clashes with the virtues of love are not from the "God of Love" because His Will to man is the "Philosophy of Love."

Jesus never professed to be God, but His followers believed, and Christians today believe, that Jesus was another rebirth of God. They ignored how often He stated in His preachings that of Himself He could do nothing, but everything He did was the workings of His Father. When He said, "I and my Father are One," He was talking about the Word of God, which He received through the Holy Spirit. In His heart He knew He was speaking the divine truth and nobody, not even the threat to His life, could stop Him with His message.

We shall also remember His statement to us in John 8:51: "Verily, verily, I say unto you, If a man keep my saying, he shall never see death." Here He talks about the survival of the soul of man contrary to the belief of many Christians. In John 14:12, it states: "Verily, verily, I say unto you, He that believeth on me, the works that I do shall he do also; and greater works than these shall he do; because I go unto my Father."

He was a man inspired by the Holy Spirit who taught Him all the works, and He suggests that we can do likewise,

3

even greater things, He said, because He did not pretend to be God at any time during His life. His teaching of love was His primary goal, and it had to be brought to the world in bits and pieces because of the low morality standards of His time. A total change to the "God of Love" would not have been received at all, especially in the synagogues of His time.

Things have changed drastically in our age because of a higher level of education. Humanity rebels against dictatorship, and there is inequality of the sexes and racial discrimination. We demand more justice in our courts and more truth and knowledge from our religions. People of today want facts and figures that they can apply to everyday life. They also want a God of influence while still alive, not only after death, as religion wants us to believe. We are told that a seat in heaven is only granted if we live according to God's Will; therefore, it is important for us to know what God's Will is so that we can live accordingly.

Salvation is not dictated by God. It has to be initiated by us so that we can benefit from the glory of God, thereby cooperating with the Holy Spirit. It has been given to me, and stressed, to apply the spiritual mixing bowl to everything we do. This will keep us observant of the virtues that Jesus talked about, toward perfection for the human being. The spiritual mixing bowl acts as the separator. By injecting love into our thoughts, it will expose evil for discard and enhance morality for living the "Philosophy of Love." Once you become accustomed to its use, you will find virtue and truth your companions and never feel alone again. The aura of the Holy Spirit will make you aware and impart to you the strength to become a better person. With this knowledge no man will ever deceive you again with false gods and prophets because you will know, first hand, that the Will of God and His divine flow has no other equal.

"God of Love" has only been taught by Jesus and has

been neglected ever since. I feel very honored to be entrusted with this divine message of how we can use the free will from God effectively. I am also the first person to tell you that the Holy Spirit is solely the carrier of good and is incapable of transmitting any evil in thoughts or actions. It was also impressed upon me that only the worldly spirit is the carrier of good and evil and would be unable to express itself in the realm of spiritual dimension. That is why the soul ego is invisible on this earth and can only express itself through a mortal body as a duality we call the living soul. This wonderful creation is endowed with what we call the free will, as mentioned above, and it is said to be a gift of God. As we know, it is supposed to sort out a selection of choices that are filling our minds, but instead our sensual instinct, alone, is guiding us into the future. The harvest without the participation of love has devastated mankind for thousands of years.

Our history books are telling us the story, and all around us life today is still dismal. With signs of war, hunger, and tribulation in every direction we care to look and listen, the question arises, "What can we do about it?" To bring the human race out of these destructive practises, there is a way to change direction whereby the ego may gain confidence and respect again. Our ruling instinct must be infused with love. The "Philosophy of Love" is the only action that can change our destiny. The educational system must adapt to the Philosophy of Love so that true values and the Will of God are being practised.

Our education today is directed toward the god of mammon in order to achieve the goals of power and wealth. Without it our chances are slim in this world, and so is respect. Regretfully, this trend does not only affect our politicians and economy, it is also a way of life in religions. Their money collections in the name of God and Jesus are astronomical. If those riches were applied to reduce the hunger in this world, truth would be smiling.

Where do these fortunes go? It is evident that luxuries of every kind are indulged, and that every famous TV preacher is supporting a glorified university in his name. I am told that these universities represent a future security for the church because it is expected that each graduate will eventually contribute ten percent of his or her income. Not a bad business return in the name of the Lord!

TV evangelists seldom preach the word of Jesus: "Sufficient into this day is the evil thereof," but we cannot deny those words have proven true for many of those in sheep's clothing. Some have fallen from the highest pedestals of high glory to the lowest of human dignity. Pride and greed will continue to take their toll, and the mighty pillars built to the god of mammon will crumble into dust. The cherished lofty praying towers of those holy men are splitting at the seams under the weight of gold, every grain of which was asked in the name of Jesus and God. Shame for all who preach for the glory of mammon. What a pity for them because I am told the only treasures for heaven are in word and action and must reflect the Will of God, which is represented only in the Philosophy of Love.

Jesus, the Christ, the greatest prophet who ever lived, the one blessed by the Holy Ghost, brought to us the teachings from the God of Love. The great principles of the laws of God are hidden in His gospel and will shine like glittering stars for those who seek in earnest. The false accusations arising from the transgression of Eve must be reversed because women have suffered unjustly ever since. Many important teachings of Jesus are misinterpreted, therefore making them more difficult to understand. How can worldly and spiritual pollution be stopped? Can peace on earth be achieved, and how?

Once you have read this book, it will put you on the threshold of a new era, a new beginning, and a new hope. In your heart a flame will rekindle, and your soul will make you conscious of your "being." The spiritual mixing bowl will assist you in balancing your body and soul and whatever else you shall find while reading this book. Heaven knows, I searched for the truth. John 14:26 states: "But the Comforter, which is the Holy Ghost, whom the Father will send in my name, He shall teach you all things, and bring all things to your remembrance, whatsoever I have said unto you." Because He said, "Ask and it shall be given unto you," I believe in His words and ask endless questions about things mankind craved to know since the beginning of time.

For forty years I explored the wilderness of the religious scene of man to find the God of Love. The promises of Jesus came true for me through believing His teachings that the Comforter will enlighten us of all things. My prayers for more light and love have been answered. Universal laws and principles of great spiritual importance were given to me in visions in the glory of spiritual dimension. I claim all the universal laws and principles in this book to be inspirations from the Holy Spirit. Many religious people will protest some of my interpretations of the Bible, and it will probably shake the foundation of fundamentalism, but I affirm from the bottom of my heart nothing in this book was the result of my own imagination. My protest that this divine message be delivered by a more gifted person went unheeded. Here I am bringing the world a message from the Holy Spirit, which is the only way to everlasting peace for the human race.

Love was the beginning of creation.
Love must stir again in the heart of man.
Love is the gift and glory of God Almighty,
Love is what life was meant to be.

This book is highly concentrated; each chapter could be enlarged into a book of its own. However, it is the author's purpose and intent to have this philosophy revealed in a condensed, truthful, and intelligible manner for anyone to read and understand. It will expose my readers to an awareness of the effects of the continuous captivating statements of facts and figures that persistently interfere with our lives. The message will loosen the grip of the worldly demons and hopefully bring light to those who seek in earnest. You will find encouragement to search within yourself and to resurrect your soul so that the Holy Spirit can inspire you to live in the Philosophy of Love.

1

Searching for the "God of Love"

The resounding echo of the demands of so many religions, "only to believe and not to question," has successfully been overcome in my heart and soul. It is this decree of religion that has kept its followers from finding their own potential for communication with their God. Such denial is contrary to the cosmos and opposed to the teachings of Jesus Christ, which many of them pretend to follow. Surely every Christian is aware that He encouraged us to ask and to question, and the Truth, He said, will then be opened unto us. In my search for the God of Love, I had many encounters with religions that still have the gods of old enshrined in stone. Their dogmas, they claim, are infallible and therefore never have to be changed. However, love does not shine forth and, mostly, it is only ingrained habitual devotion to old-time traditions that keeps followers content.

The last hundred years of industrial revolution have dramatically changed many nations of this world. The increasing educational standards have hardened mankind against individual self-expression of their being. Bigotry is the tool that buries the truth regardless of which institution's dogmas are being practised, but slowly people have gathered the courage to defend their own inspired opinions. The gradual freedom of expression is starting to tear the yoke off mental slavery and if we follow the Philosophy of Love theme, then the salvation of all life on this planet will have begun. The greatest achievement for the living soul is to accomplish harmony in all and for all; this would be the sweet fruit ripened by the Holy Spirit. It could be achieved by all of humanity if we begin our search by first putting our feet firmly on the threshold of truth. The spiritual mixing bowl can be our measure for making the choices for us to live by.

We must reach beyond the gods of good and evil so that we can understand and comprehend the difference between the worldly spirit and the Holy Spirit. Teachings of a God in the far reaches of the heavens seem to distance Him from us according to our worldly perception, and His assumed temper and predilection for fierce punishments has resulted in jittery fears instead of love. Such an image of God constituted a curtain of evil, used for thousands of years by the kings and unsavory prophets to camouflage their own wickedness. Until this day we hear them preaching that just about everything is an act of God and—oh yes—whatever happens is God's plan! Even all our actions, most religions preach, are the result of it.

I can tell you in all honesty in the name of the Holy Spirit that we are solely responsible for all happenings amongst us. It is our privilege to be aware of God's presence if we so choose and to resurrect our soul to its rightful place. Under His guiding light, we are inclined to do the honorable thing; therefore He is working with us but not for us, as generally assumed.

In my search for the God of Love, I was compelled to study a great variety of occult literature that was available. Together with my wife, I joined different churches, temples, revival crusades, meditation movements, as well as a mystical organization. Astrology and numerology were not left out, and I read about the beliefs of most major religions. The road grew longer as the time passed and there was no end in sight, but my strong desire to find never faltered. Somehow I had a feeling that somewhere along the way I would come across a flicker of light that would point in a direction acceptable to my heart. It might be a fair summation to state that I crisscrossed the religious jungle of man for over forty years, but I finally emerged from that vast maze in ecstatic triumph.

Looking back on my childhood, I find it is important to start there because that is where my first conception of God occurred. I was born into a family of five children and raised in a small town in the Austrian Alps. With parents of little means but towers of love, we had a happy childhood in the midst of a friendly and generous community. Most of the population existed on small holdings sufficient to support one to ten cows—and I loved to work for our neighbors whenever possible, planting, harvesting, gardening, tending cows, and chopping wood for fuel. The reward for working was usually paid in farm produce, which I proudly took home. Most of the people I worked for gave a customary thank-you prayer before every main meal, a tradition probably dating back for generations. We were a totally Catholic parish, with some very religious people, and every Sunday the church would be full to overflowing. Going to church was a must for children; only sickness would be an excuse for absence. The school curriculum included Catholic instruction twice a week. This was a prominent subject on the report card.

Mother taught us to pray, I am sure, as soon as we were born and succeeded well in making us believe in Jesus. There were also many saints in the lower ranks and, of course, Holy Mary, the mother of Jesus, was also mentioned in prayer. There were many religious holidays throughout the year, and—as you can probably see by now—my childhood had absolutely no shortage of religious indoctrination. We had a typical childhood. We believed sincerely in all the doctrines

11

and traditions that we were taught and looked up to the priest as a man of God who knew all the secrets of heaven. Thus in my naive little heart, mythology was fact. It was the job of the Christ Child to decorate the tree and to bring all the presents on Christmas Eve and rewards were given according to behavior during the year.

Deep in my heart there lingered some resentment and disappointment when my friends were showered with more and better gifts than my own. I even knew that some of them had told lies, but considered myself without blemish and therefore felt I should have fared much better! Somehow my disappointment was never discussed with my parents because deep down my feelings told me it would hurt them and they would rightfully consider me a selfish boy.

After seeing injustice all around, a little rebellion kindled inside me, so one day I collected my courage to talk to our priest. Somehow I expected him to know what the saints, Jesus, or God would do about this. My problems poured out of my mouth while he was listening, and by the time his answer was given, my self-esteem sank to its lowest level. I still remember the stern voice that told me to never, ever question God or the actions of the church because these constitute the greatest sin that you can commit. God knows what He is doing and we are here just to believe and not to question. My heart was crushed, and I felt empty and despised. All along I believed in true communion with the holy ones above, and now I found myself a heartbroken stranger with no right to question the important virtues in life. Somehow the spiritual flame in this child's heart, and the trust acquired, started to fade away because unfairness from above was not accepted in my heart.

As time passed, church attendance became a chore and my religious observances a forced habit. I still continued to pray, because it was hard to shake an indoctrinated belief in

God, no matter how blunted I felt. With time I started to realize that the people around the community were mostly just habitual churchgoers. Many attended church to be seen and to show off their new clothes. It was an excellent place to talk business and to meet old friends. Occasionally we visited the graves of deceased family members. The church music and choir, I must say, were very pleasant and refreshing to listen to, despite my otherwise deteriorating attachment.

One year during the school holidays, my mother asked me to accompany her to a distant mountain valley to visit family friends. This was a treat that my mother always looked forward to once or twice a year. My parents maintained a large vegetable garden at that time, so all kinds of fresh produce were prepared to be taken along on this long trek. My job was to be the donkey to pull the wagon. At our destination were longtime friends of my mother, a large family with seven children. They looked forward just as much to receiving our goods as we in return anticipated carrying home their fresh farm produce.

We departed early in the morning and would arrive there much later in the day. Any of you who have travelled such stretches and are familiar with those tiny mountain grottoes or chapels, doubtless know that maybe no more than four to six people can be accommodated on a kneeling bench. These were built especially for hikers such as we were seeking to find a few minutes of restful solitude along the lonely stretches of winding roads. Mother loved those places and would not pass one without spending fifteen or twenty minutes at prayer. She would emerge with a glow of happiness, totally refreshed, and would never fail to sing along the way to preserve our good spirits.

Upon our return trip, a few days later, Mother repeated her visit to the grottoes. I questioned her for the first time and asked, "Why do you spend so much time in these small empty chapels instead of attending church on Sunday where people can see how good you are, and God might be there too instead of here in this small and lonely place?" A protest accompanied her disappointed expression. She replied, "You know very well that I have to cook dinner on Sundays." I wish to explain that every Sunday at 1:00 P.M. was dinnertime, and for most people, it was the best meal of the week and the occasion for a family gathering. Our mother had a good excuse for staying home for this big feast. Thus many women attended early mass instead.

I believe Mother relished the idea of staying home so that she could have her own way of communion in solitude. Finally her face mellowed, and she confided that she disliked the long and drawn-out rituals of Sunday Mass and preferred to commune with God in peace and quiet by herself at home. "God is in my heart, and He is present everywhere we go," she said. "In this little grotto is peace and quiet where I find tranquillity and dignity. People do not have to see me in prayer; such intimate moments are between God and me," she exclaimed. I felt sheepish, and at the same time astounded, that Mother actually and truly believed in a God here and now in her presence rather than an unapproachable God somewhere beyond our horizons. A proud feeling for her innate wisdom began to stir within me, and later on in life, the same convictions became a part of me.

During my adolescence, World War II was raging out of control. When I reached age seventeen, my health was tested by the government agents and the military to prepare me to fight for the country. By this time the whole world was in turmoil and all major countries around the globe had their production lines going day and night, spewing out destructive monstrosities for the air, sea, and land. Eventually they reached their capacity to destroy not only the enemy but the world itself. By the time I made it to the frontier as a trained soldier in 1943, evidence clearly showed that the oversized battle zones could not be defended successfully. Fate had already decided our downfall, and we were at the mercy of time. Where and when the end would come was the secret of stupidity. World War II surely the most extensive and destructive event in the memory of man. In such testing times of tribulation, hunger, rape, torture, disease, and killing throughout the battle zones, is it fair to ask, "Where is God"? Experiencing war with every fibre of my body, and witnessing the suffering of victims, my heart was often overwhelmed in agony and fear and would cry out, "Peace to the world," in the hope of bridging the enormous abyss of hell created by mankind. My heart, however, was hardened to cope with the continuous onslaught of terror and finally, after spending three years as a soldier and one year in a prisoner-of-war camp, I succeeded in escaping, which ended my experience of war.

I reached home in May 1946 and was blessed to come upon all of my family, my parents, two sisters and two brothers gathered at home around the table having lunch. We were a very fortunate family because my two older brothers, my father and I returned from the war unscathed, which fills me with a joyful wonder to this day. God knows that I had anger in me, and it took a while to become free of its haunting presence. My whole teenage years between seventeen and twenty-one, until I came home from the war, was an existence of horror and exasperation. Being on the side of the losers made it even worse because blame reduced one's self-esteem, and this was very demeaning.

When meeting some relatives of old friends who had been killed during the war, I could sense their hearts being torn apart by questioning as to why their brothers or sons had not come home. I was able to sympathize with them in their grief, but as for myself, I realized how lucky I actually was to be there alive. Since then I look upon each day as borrowed time. The past years have told me how cheaply life has been treated by mankind and how enormous has become the scope of evil that has spread around the world. In tribulation the question always arises again and again, "Where is God or where was He? If He does exist, what role is He playing concerning humanity?" The churches are again full of people praying, but the wickedness did not subside with the end of World War II.

My destiny has taken me on a journey across the sea, and a new era in my life started with this fresh beginning. It was my intention to bury and leave behind the wicked past, and with it the old belief of the dual God of good and evil, the one who will inflict pestilence, revenge, and jealousy. He is the God of many religions, but that misinterpretation has absolutely no place in my heart. Such man-made perceptions are the creations of evil, and void of love and do not compliment the God they claim possesses love. These kinds of mental shackles, I vowed, would not be part of my new beginning. I trusted love for guidance and soon became aware that no spiritual message is true if it is void of love. My newfound confidence instilled strength and constancy into my heart for the search, and I was pointed in the direction of the "God of Love."

In 1952 I landed on this great continent of North America and settled in the good land of Canada where I was able to raise a family in peace. My avocation continued in my sincere and persistent search for the "God of Love," and the momentum increased year by year. This country has people of many races and a great choice of religious organizations from around the world. It was here, as time passed by, that I studied the Bible and a great deal of other literature. Together with my wife, I attended various church services with an open mind, seeking signs of the God of Love.

Disappointment was never far away because the restrictions of religious dogmas and their established boundaries gives one the feeling that all sheep, once they are corralled, walk in circles. It is their hope that after death, at sometime further on, there will occur physical resurrection, but they are uncertain whether or not they will fit into heaven or hell. All those who died since the very beginning are according to the teachings, apparently still waiting! I cannot see love or justification here, and there is absolutely no reason for God to have such a useless plan.

Billions of people would have to be resurrected all at once, so shouldn't we ask the question, "Why?" After that they are supposed to live on this tiny planet forever; and the ones who are defective and old, what about them, would they enjoy it? Such a materialistic philosophy is depressing and not at all consistent with the rhythm of the universe nor with the God of Love. Why should He bury for so long his treasures who were the godly and deserving people?

Please read what Jesus had to say in John 8:51: "Verily, verily, I say unto you, If a man keep my saying, he shall never see death." His comment of never seeing death was strictly meant for the spiritual soul, not our physical body. This applies to physical resurrection as envisioned and preached by religion. There is too much emptiness in such a belief of dormancy and emphasis on the physical dead body, whereas universal spiritual laws make much more sense for us to live by.

Take note of Origen, the great Christian theologian and philosopher of the Roman Church who made the following statement regarding ascension (referring to Saint John 20:17): "The ascent of the son to the father must be understood with holy insight in the ways of God, and we must realize it is the ascent of mind rather than of the body, as widely believed." This foregoing comment tells us that opinions varied greatly among the early church fathers.

We once attended one of the great revival crusades under a big tent in Stampede Park in Calgary. Thousands and thousands of people flocked to this great event, from which the afflicted and sick were hoping to walk away healed. Rows upon rows were waiting for miracles to happen, and as the excitement heightened, people were told to accept Christ as their Savior. That apparently, was the appropriate moment for the climax of the gathering.

I believe the purpose of this crusade was to auction Jesus for money! The preacher's voice echoed through the massive crowds: "If you love Jesus, show it to Him. There will be plate collections coming your way; please give generously. Don't you think Jesus is worth twenty dollars? Reach deeply into your pockets because you might find thirty or fifty dollars! If you love Him, nothing is too much for Jesus. Remember, He will give it back to you tenfold. God bless you all for your generosity."

I felt great disappointment because anyone giving less would have felt cheap, and those who believed that the money was really going to Jesus were cheated under false pretenses. Collecting money and offerings in the name of God is a trick as old as man himself. We read in the old Scriptures that God Himself set the price of His services. In those days He only accepted the best without any blemishes. Later on we read that He led His chosen people into wars, and the spoils thereof were commanded to be brought into His treasury. Such was the bounty of the gods of the times.

Appeasing atonements are a carry-over into the churches of today. Still, we are told that we are giving it to God with a promise of a tenfold return. This untruth and the greed of man will sacrifice the principle of love on every turn.

Such a wolf in sheep's clothing fasted and prayed in his ivory tower, his purpose being to raise millions of dollars or God, he claimed, would take his life. There are unlimited claims for using the name of God for raising money, but accusing Him of killing for money is the extreme of Christian deception. The great multitude who saved his life from the killer God hopefully came to realize that his message came from the god of mammon, whom this man is representing, and had nothing to do with Jesus Christ. The cause of his plea was not for the hungry and the destitute of this world, but to inject money into a university project.

Such things belong to the rich man's domain, and of course I understand the worldly importance of this man's church. It is more profitable to groom professionals in an institution of higher learning because its graduates are expected to bring in an eventual clone return of ten percent, a far better investment than one in the poor of this world. Well, this pretentious holy man certainly knows how to get money out of people's pockets, so maybe he should be hired by the government to use his tricks when it needs more taxes!

The pharaohs and kings had their own way of collecting. They just slaughtered a neighboring tribe in the name of God and took everything they had. This is how Solomon obtained his riches and slaves to build his two temples and to expand his empire. The Old Testament is the witness to what transpired in those days, and love was never a contributing factor.

I read that an elderly lady willed her home prematurely into the godly hands of her favorite church. An unexpected sickness depleted her funds, and when she asked for help, they refused. Upon her taking the matter to court, the court ruled that she could not retract a donation to her church. Now for such churches Jesus had this to say in Mark 12:40: "which devour widows' houses, and for a pretence make long prayers: these shall receive greater damnation."

Strangely I have never heard this quote in sermons about unholy collection practices, which happen so frequently; however, could it be perhaps that such truth would destroy the glory and effect of the prayers to the god of mammon? You hypocrites with fancy cars and you castle collectors! You are preaching in the name of Jesus Christ who taught His followers to distribute their riches amongst the poor, to take only one coat and follow Him. You are collecting donations in His name to invest in all kinds of businesses, real estate, and savings accounts. Is it because you do not trust His teachings?

Remember, He taught that the morrow will take care of itself and those who believe will feed you. I challenge all Christian religious organizations, churches, cults, and TV evangelists around the world to see if they could face Jesus today with their bulging bank accounts. Remember, this would save many people from starvation on this planet. Thousands are dying every day and children are still being prostituted, and you let it happen. Where is love, I ask, and where is justice? Take note, ye preachers of God and their followers: do you think collected donations are furthering the Word of God by creating golden monsters? No, by such works you have done nothing but deprive the poor and destitute children of this world. Instead, give your money to the International Red Cross or similar worldly organizations if you want to help the cause of Jesus and the God of Love.

Consider the history of people with primitive religions. They were called heathens, but most of them worshiped their idols in honesty. Their beliefs, derived from ancestral and totem spirits, were those of primitive people who did not fail in sincerity and often carried more credibility than many religions today. For example, a deity is born because of a person's spectacular experience in life. He venerated a great courageous and powerful spirit of a great bear, and he bestowed this upon his first son and history was born into the family. The bear's head will grace the family's totem pole, and to keep this belief alive a tradition will grow to appease this great spirit at certain times of the year and communion according to the need of the person is established.

Such a totem spirit could derive from practically any powerful or beautiful phenomenon by which those people were impressed. There are endless possibilities for veneration: the heavenly bodies, animals, birds, fish, the elements or associated forces, such as hurricanes, thunder, lightning, rushing rivers, tidal waves, fires, and not least the spirits of their ancestors. Make no mistake, if their contentions were complimentary to love, then the Holy Spirit would not fail to bless them.

In studying religion we become quickly aware of the first commandment: "The Lord alone shall be exalted." It is the praise and the mandate of the prophets, and it remains the first requirement of every cult and religion. This behest was not about the decision of the people, but was preconceived and enforced by the rulers and their prophets. The free will of the masses was destroyed by force and slavery. Women had no rights as chattels of men, and men, in turn, were the property of the war lords. Beliefs and religion, therefore, were not practiced by choice as we experience them today. There are still many such countries under similar rule where women are still mere chattel easily abused, traded or sold. Also, children are still used for slave labour in many such countries, and no religion has fought for their freedom. Women have no say in religion either. It is only a short while since the first few were ordained as ministers here in the West; otherwise, they have no such acceptance the world over.

21

Today, especially in North America, we like to believe that religion was always an institution for God and of God consisting of preaching love. Nothing could be further from the truth, and it was disappointing to my heart, and it will be astonishing to everyone's mind and soul to find out the truth behind the veil and see revealed what the foundations of our old-time religions were built on. The foundations were not love nor were they justice; they were fashioned of power and greed for entrapping the unwary of the world. They were designed by the kings who ruled the prophets, seers, and astrologers to construct a constitution so that they could force every body and soul in his empire to obey. We do know that the alternative to obeying was torture and death, and that this description of horror is not a fantasy of mine but is well documented in the Old Testament.

Out of those scriptures arose three major religions of this world descended from the time of Abraham. His first son, whose name was Ishmael, was born to Hagar and from this son was born the great religion of Islam. The second son was born to Sarah and was called Isaac, and from his birth resulted another great religion called Judaism. After the death of Jesus, a new doctrine was born called Christianity, which includes various religions and sects comprising one third of the world's population.

The teachings of this great religion related back to Abraham through the branch of Isaac when revolutionary views and changes were made by the teachings of Christ. For the first time in history, religious followers were encouraged to live according to the Word of God, which He proclaimed was love. His teachings comprise the Philosophy of Love whereby those who practice it have repented and refrained from evil. Such redemption of us was the dream of His mission, which He ultimately hoped to achieve and for which cause His life was taken.

22

According to His inspiring doctrine, I do believe He was the greatest among living souls, having experienced the continuous spark of the Holy Spirit. There is no one who holds Him dearer to the truth than I, but nevertheless there has never been—and never will be—a mortal creation to fill the shoes of the God of Love. Exaltation to this God can only come from within our soul through the light of love, never by the command or force of man nor by the lords of evil.

Strife around the world is continuing, and the echo of war is menacing people at any given hour somewhere on this planet. It is such uncertainty and evil tidings that arouse the question in us, "Is this all there is to life what we are witnessing at present?" Taking this query seriously, I was ready for a thorough soul-searching, and I wondered if I was being hypocritical and dodging the truth instead of facing the reality regarding God. In view of human misery and the open blame that God is the instigator of all things, is it not fair to speculate why the whole world is built on injustice?

Religion has taught us for centuries that whatever happens is the Will of God and that He alone is the master of our destiny, regardless of our self-determination. Searching in my soul for the connection of this relationship, I found the teachings of Jesus to be in stark contrast to the fatalistic belief above. "Seek and ye shall find, knock and it shall be opened, ask and it shall be given unto you"—those heralding principles urge us to the very use of self-determination. Jesus tells us to follow in His footsteps (commandments) and everything else will be added unto us. He is ever encouraging us to believe that our efforts could surpass His accomplishments because His life will be shortened. He then proclaims that in love all things are fulfilled.

This array of wisdom shows us the path He followed. Our personal destiny then reverts onto our own responsibility, and a new law of creation takes over. "Ye shall reap as ye have sown": nothing could be more explicit than this universal law that our seeds will bear the fruits of tomorrow. In spite of all the effort that Jesus put behind His doctrine, which He claims to have received from the God of Love, the twisting and turning of words and the rewriting of the Bible, the preaching from the pulpits, and the changed interpretation of parables have greatly diluted the spiritual content of His Philosophy of Love. This is the lifestyle that Jesus wanted the human race to follow and is the very cause for which He sacrificed His life. With so many references to Jesus stressing the actions of love, no one person can call himself or herself a Christian without practising His doctrine with all his or her body and soul.

The depth to which I explored brought to light the method by which to unravel and comprehend the unpredictable behavior of a human being. His turbulent lifestyle was not caused by the influence of God but rather by the lack of it. God is blamed, thereby relieving guilty parties of their responsibility for guiding their living souls along the path towards a lifestyle of love. Instead, the worldly spirit has fashioned mankind for thousands of years according to its five sensual desires. And religions, too, were growing fat on their bounties.

Jesus's arrival and His courage were to break this spell, but the inherent confusion between good and evil has not yet been sorted out of the holy books and dogmas of man's secret enclaves. Yes, our sensual body can live without the designated knowledge of the Holy Spirit, but this lifestyle has given mankind hell on earth. The Philosophy of Love has not been taught by religion nor by educators, and until such time as this happens, the Redeemer will not have had His day of glory on this earth. Because of it, I have made a pledge to my soul to leave no stone unturned until the day I have heralded to the world the existence of the God of Love. His will is manifested unto us by the Holy Spirit in the vitality of the Philosophy of Love.

Resolution

Our minds are loaded with hardship and sorrow,
Regardless, we like to see the sun rise again tomorrow.
To experience anew and try our best for another day,
Not to give up but to approach life's mysteries in a new
way.

Enlightenment is a state of awareness, the unfolding of truth for the living soul in relation to the established universal laws. The fruit of life was meant to be love; likewise, destiny is a time plan to achieve harmony, and no other outcome can unfold unto us the mysteries from beyond. Love is easily imagined but hard to fulfill because of the dominant translations of the five senses. Without having understanding of the sixth sense, and without input from the spiritual soul, love is put at risk of being used by opportunists rather than being known as a way of life. The mixing bowl will always make you aware of the need to balance life. Your destiny will generously bring forth the seeds of righteous deeds.

GUIDE TO THE
"PHILOSOPHY OF LOVE"

Resurrection of Your Soul
Salvation to Humanity

Performance

1. Place thoughts and plans into mixing bowl.
2. Pray for love to be injected into the bowl.
3. Thoughts and love are mixed.
4. Pray until evil is made obvious so it can be discarded.
5. This separation brings forth the wholesome thoughts and plans to be used.
6. With practice, the actions will be free of evil and complementary with the virtues of love.

The above six steps comprise the workings of the spiritual mixing bowl.

7. Pray for more light and love which will strengthen a person's resolve.
8. With the above interactions of the mixing bowl, when goodness wins, then the "Philosophy of Love" has been achieved.
9. The awareness and actions of love have resurrected the soul.
10. Salvation is in effect according to righteousness.
11. Finding truth within, "Ask and it shall be given."
12. Honest desire for truth has overcome the worldly spirit, and the divine flow has balanced the body and soul.

All our thought processes should filter through the spiritual mixing bowl. During general conversations we can experience the presence of spiritual love guiding our thoughts. Important decisions take time; therefore we should follow the six steps described in the preceding paragraph.

Step 1. By placing our idea into the imaginary spiritual

mixing bowl, we momentarily part from our possessive influence of sentiment. This will more readily highlight the evil to be discarded because we can analyse this process from the outside. Subsequently, it will draw us like a magnet to wrongful dealings, evilness against others, or to our environment. Political decisions should be cleansed by spiritual love because they are very important to everyone. Through this process religion would shine with absolute truth, and the teachings of a wrathful God would be the crumbs for Satan. Faith, to be meaningful, must find spiritual love; otherwise, its effect will be useless. Many people claim to have inspirations, visions, and apparitions with various emotional experiences. However, they must all withstand the test above in order to shine of truth and love or be discarded. This housecleaning of our worldly spirit is essential for us in every walk of life. The application of the spiritual mixing bowl will give us confidence, happiness, and a sincere lifestyle in the Philosophy of Love. Love is the Redeemer of the world and enables human beings to have another chance to widen the narrow road toward harmony and peace.

My Prayer to the God of Love

God of Love, come into us,
Give us more light and more Love.
Inspire us to balance our body and soul,
That we can fulfill Your Will
In the Philosophy of Love.

A prayer between God and man is personal, more often than not a cry for help. During the past forty years, the above prayer served me well in the resurrection of my soul. I can only encourage my readers to do the same. Use my prayer if you so desire, or devise your own according to your needs.

In whatever way you knock or ask on the heavenly door in sincerity, you will not be disappointed. "Seek and ye shall find" is a principle in the Book of Life, and it will be opened unto you. In the above prayer, you may notice the word *us* because personally I feel selfish asking for favors of God for myself; therefore, I hope "us" will reach even beyond the circle of my loved ones.

A prayer is ringing the bells from the depth of our soul, and its echo will be acknowledged by the Holy Spirit.

Prayer is not a means to an end because it activates a new beginning. Through prayer we will receive spiritual inspirations, but if we neglect or don't understand them, then the answers to prayers will be lost and in vain. The Holy Spirit acts according to our needs, and our soul will enlighten us thereof in a manner that will resolve our problems. That is how God works with us, but not for us, and we have proof to that effect in our everyday life. Allow me to repeat that all the prayers in this world will be for naught if we don't listen and follow the guidance of the Holy Spirit.

Prayers are greatly affected by certain principles of the spiritual domain. We should be aware that paid prayers or paid traditions or any other worldly donations will reach no further than the benefactors of your money. There is a spiritual law that only prayers out of love and truth will find the connection to the Holy Spirit.

2

Awakening

Since the day of the eerie sound of the jungle drums proclaiming the ritual dance of a bloodthirsty tribe, its neighbors knew their days were numbered. Hence, the struggle for survival of mankind had its tragic beginning.

The vast expansion of plains, bush country, and the seas, with their substantial food supplies, were insufficient for this greedy species called "man." Population, as yet, was merely a handful on this beautiful self-sufficient planet Earth. As the sunrises passed, man continued to be his own destructive enemy because fear and greed were an inheritance and a way of life.

The influential beauty of nature and its laws touched many a man's heart, but unfortunately they were mostly abused by its inhabitants. Spiritual influences were recognized by early man, but their role of application ended in the selfish purpose of self-glorification. Their faith, therefore, that the conquerors were protected by their spirit, made them believe that they were the chosen people of God. Arrogant beliefs that such a God meddled in all their affairs and gave them protection in thievery, murder, and right down to wars were quite acceptable, and I must confess with horror, even to this day, such was the game of past civilizations, which we now call history.

In ancient scrolls there were references to organized religions, which actually gave us insight into their philosophies of a few thousand years past. Some of the oldest religions still in existence today were founded within the past few thousand years. We all know that Christianity is one of the great and largest religions of our time, and the Bible is the fundamental doctrine thereof. Some of the oldest religions are Hinduism, Judaism, Buddhism, and Islam—only to name a few. It is interesting to note that those old-time religions have fragmented into hundreds of splinter groups of various cults and sects. Literally thousands of those organizations are influencing the human race at any given time throughout the world, with messages to man from all the prophets of the past who inspired religion. The most renowned of these were Abraham, Jesus, Krishna, Buddha, Muhammad, and many others. Fundamentally they had great similarities. For example, their teachings of the "one God principle" differed only in the pleasures they attributed to the god of their time.

"Ye shall reap as ye have sown" is a principle and law as old as nature, which has never changed and never will. The significance of this holy principle tells us to sow only the good seed, but this was badly neglected by religion, and the fruits thereof have to be harvested by each and every generation. This harvesting will continue to take its course. Nature's laws and principles must be obeyed by man if he chooses to survive on this planet. Long biographies in Holy scriptures about "all-inspired man" are most interesting to read for passing the time, but in doing so the real message for man's survival to learn and obey the laws and principles of nature is thereby diluted and misunderstood. Evidence of this fact is clearly seen by every open-minded person. It is written, "Seek and ye shall find" in Matthew 7:7–8, and yet religion taught me "only to believe" and "not to question."

The honorable bishop of London, Canada, said it best: The teachings of the Church must be considered on a "take it or leave it" basis and not be subject to questions. He reasoned that the essence of faith is precise acceptance—acceptance without question. Jesus, however, did not accept the dogma of His Synagogue; in Matthew 15:3–9, He complained that they were full of man-made laws: "But in vain they do worship me, teaching for doctrines the commandments of men." Would you question the faith of Jesus because He criticized the teachings of His Synagogue? Why should we be restricted to blind acceptance? Is it not time to overcome this rot of darkness and bring forth more and new light from the temple of God from within (1 Cor. 3:16–17)?

Religious dogmas were created in such a manner that the followers had to have only that foregoing obligation to be a passive member for qualifying. The chores of seeking were already done by the founder of their doctrine and accepted as the ultimate truth. The foundation of every religion was thereby weakened, right from the beginning of its spiritual purpose. "Seek and ye shall find" would become automatically obsolete and therefore, by accepting the dogma of "believing" and not "questioning," which necessitates the rules for each member, it becomes a mere spiritual monopoly and slavery. Habitual participation is established, and no further inquiry of the great mystery of whence man came and his final destination is given a second thought, nor taught.

The free will of man is a gift from God, so they say, but do we fully understand its use? The words imply multiple choices of right and wrong, and this is where the problems begin. In order to make these choices, we have to comprehend the right from the wrong, and the good from the evil. Unless we have established guidelines for comparison for the continuous thought process of our worldly spirit, which is the carrier of good and evil, we cannot fully appreciate these things.

On the other hand, the Holy Spirit carries the Philosophy

of Love, which is only good. Knowing the functions of the only two existing spirits in this universe will make it much easier for us to select choices and be aware of the fruit they may bear. The formula is simple: the Holy Spirit carries Love and must blend with all the virtues of Love, whereas the worldly spirit or sensual force is a carrier of good and evil, often clashing with the virtues of Love. Instinct is not reliable because it is the foundation of the sensual spirit, where truth becomes flawed and greed and power are the glory of its goal.

During my early search for the God of Love, I was made aware of the great differences between the two existing spirits, and I was guided toward the use of the spiritual mixing bowl. It is a tool for us to balance our body and soul and is the guiding light to master the Philosophy of Love. Do not forget that Jesus said, "On the fruit ye shall know them, and there is no sweeter than Love."

The God-given free will of man is not an assumption but a living fact; therefore, contrary to an enclosed environment of organized religion, there is no end to the search into self and the unknown spiritual realm of God. Free thinking is essential to explore the science of mind and soul. No true religion of God will ever have a closed chapter of free expression and thought.

Man would never have achieved space travel without the free projective thinking of scientists. On the contrary, scientists of spirituality, how far have you gone? Your fundamental beliefs have never changed since the so-called Dark Ages in which you are evidently still dwelling. The fruits thereof still reflect the same: discrimination of various kinds, wars and hatred, which are predominantly our daily dishes.

Man is a free agent and therefore not a victim of fate; he has the ability to be master of his own destiny. The choice will remain with the individual. Whatever we are doing, constant confirmations between choosing rightly or wrongly are the building blocks of our future. The consequences follow each decision automatically, hence the source for the path of our destiny. All sorrows are man-made and will have to be undone by man. Here is the place for religion to educate men of the natural and spiritual laws, which will correct our blind choices and the wrongful application of will. Never again say that our lives are predestined by fate, as we have too much proof to the contrary. Every living soul is responsible for its own destiny, and that is why we need the guidance of the Holy Spirit. The universal mind is ever ready to inspire and enlighten us through inspiration for the simple truthful asking; it is the source of spiritual education for the benefit of man. Pray for more light and love, and you will find it. The choices of actions are made by your free will, and "Ye shall reap as ye have sown" is the unchanging law of creation.

Most people in all walks of life do believe in a God of some sort. The nonbelievers also have a point when they argue, "Why would a loving God give a command to kill innocent women and children in wars as recorded in the Old Testament?" Their argument is well-founded because the warrior God, Jehovah, did not impress with love but rather with fear. Of course, the preaching that unfortunate happenings are the Will of God has not assisted to enlighten them either. The churches never blame man or themselves for their actions or lack of them, which have caused and created the problems; therefore, through the wrongful education about God, the rift began to widen. Atheism is a direct result of this failure because masses of people became tired of this uncertainty of a God and so rightly, in their opinion, denounced Him. Millions of churchgoing people believe in God today through the instilled fear of a jealous and revengeful God who will, on the last day, save or destroy them.

How, then, can these people profess to love Him if they

are actually afraid of God? Such a philosophy has been bearing its fruits into this day—consider war, famine, racial discrimination, pollution, the population explosion, only to mention a few human miseries. How easy to blame someone else and say, "It is God's Will." Religion had, at one time or another, influence on all men on this planet. If their words and actions were holy, no man would have drifted away from the magnificent and necessary relationship between God and man.

Any church or congregation with the slightest segregation or discrimination of any kind is destroying the vitality it is supposed to stand for. In God, every man is an equal, regardless of color or title. Only the actions will determine the quality of each living soul. How, then, dare you as an organization, proclaim to be righteous and look down on others and persecute those of different opinions? How can you deny somebody of a different color the ministry of your church? Why segregate, for religious reasons, little children from one community into separate schools, which illustrates to them and encourages again discrimination against others?

We can see a living example of it in many places around the world today. Why should a woman be less worthy to be a minister than a man? All these rules of churches certainly do not illustrate love to mankind. They are detrimental inventions to an otherwise healthy community. In man's environment, the teachings have to be toward universal love and unity—all for one and one for all—until such time as this happens, your words carry no spiritual meaning. It is a direct fault of the churches of the world not to educate their congregations to these needs, namely, "thou shalt love thy fellow man as thyself." There is no other commandment greater than this.

Jesus said holiness is not in big words and walking around in fancy robes pretending, but in sincere, loving actions, which will be the only way to convert the wicked beast of man to a more gentle creature. The churches are supposed to be factories to produce beauty and enlightenment for the soul. All these centuries the factories are still being built, reflecting great splendor and wealth. They are a minister's and architect's dream and accomplishment where new expansion programmes are added to take care of the dancing, dining and games. In the meantime, they have forgotten their purpose. What was to be the product? Saint Luke 12:34 states: "For where your treasure is, there will be your heart also."

Religion of tomorrow will have to be experiencing God, which is the most important thing of all. If you cannot achieve it, preaching and wishful thinking about it is a mere pastime and an entertainment on Sundays. The character of man is formed by his worldly spirit, which in generalization we can describe as being selfish at heart, domineering in behavior, but possessing a spiritual soul. If the latter is dormant, we shall have nothing left but wickedness.

Man changes his character at will, whereas an animal lives by its instinct according to the beast; therefore, the wickedness of man can be meaner than that of any beast. We are the sole agents of balancing our bodies and souls with the right mixture, which is obtained through our free will. The goodness in our spiritual soul can be tapped to our need and allowed to flow through our personality. Spirituality is a subject that the majority of people do not bother about, let alone question. Its definition is shrouded with mysterious associations, and yet it is as much of a necessity in life as the breathing of clean air.

The more a man becomes conscious of it, the more light he might see. Love and understanding increases, and finally peaceful coexistence with nature is found. This will awaken man to the wisdom of its laws and principles. The holiest achievement that the living soul can obtain on this planet is harmony with all; only then can man claim to have a resemblance to the image of God. Until such a time as this happens, man is only moving clay and not comparable with the universal mind, which is not of a shape nor of clay. God is an active spirit everywhere, and His laws are nature's laws of which we are a part. Those who obey them are honoring His creation, but any other religious teachings are secondary, which just pass the time of a bored people.

God can be experienced in many ways. The most common is that of instantaneous inspiration. The following is a good example of this. During World War II, we were stationed high in the Italian Alps and our tent was set up in the backdrop of a high hill. The enemy shells were exploding in the front or would fly over the hump. One night, as the heavy shelling continued, we were ordered to vacate our tent and find safety in rocky crevices a few hundred feet below. Soon the cold made me sneak back into the warmth of my sleeping bag in the tent where I spent all night in comfort.

At daybreak the shelling stopped and a frightening feeling started to come over me. Finally I decided to abandon the canvas for the safety of the rocks. I was about to leave when two of my colleagues came in, so I expressed my fears to them and suggested that we go back to the rocks. They were convinced that the shooting was over and commenced to light the stove. The climax came when I threw myself onto the floor. At about the same instant, the last shell of the night exploded right in front of the tent, killing my companions instantly. I am sure that most people can recall, at one time or another, an experience that they would term a sixth-sense phenomenon influencing us along the way.

Spirituality is the wavelength that transmits communication through our soul between God and man directly to our thoughts and senses. Such inspiration could be the rightful inheritance of every living soul, and this "Voice from within" is common and should be recognized as such. Our prayers and actions toward God reinforce our warning signals and enlighten us in every way, here and now, while we are still alive on this planet. God is very much with us and always has been—only our attunement is lacking because of many false religious teachings. True desire and humbleness will strengthen our action of sincerity and will pull the veil shrouded in mystery, which will bring us the life force needed for a harmonious existence.

According to our actions, it will be given unto us, and therefore man's destiny is of his own making, chosen through his God-given free will. Man has the choice to walk in His presence and gain understanding, or do it alone and drown in his own arrogance, of which we have evidence all around us. Let us stop blaming God for our misfortunes and fortunes, for bliss is neither, only the serenity of the living soul.

Try to find proof within, get conscious of His very existence, and as the years pass by, your communion will give you joy and bliss. God's mind will make itself known unto you through inspirations, dreams or visions. The cause of experiencing is action, and experiencing brings Truth. The Holy Spirit is with us at all times and only our true desire will be the medium needed to achieve harmony between body and soul.

3

Religion

A renowned clergyman of the Protestant ministry has told his ministers that what he terms a "holy burnout" has reached epidemic proportions. A recent survey by the Barna Research Group has indicated that, because of their demanding work, ministers are the most frustrated people in America. Then the reverend declared, "We feel that if we are not ministering to a large church, God is not blessing us." He says that although millions of dollars are spent annually trying to get non-Christians to respond, real church growth remains minimal. The above views, but very important messages, are afflicting religion the world over. It is only the beginning of what can happen to a religion if there is no renewal in inspiration and misunderstandings in general.

We are witnessing a drastic change in believers and nonbelievers alike because of what I mentioned previously. Self-awareness resulting from higher education is demanding more changes in our institutions. Politics for our worldly needs and seekers of the God of Love require more spiritual awareness than is demonstrated in churches everywhere. I maintain that the above problems are happening because of the neglect of the true teachings of Christ. As far as churches are concerned, my message will surely fall on deaf ears because they will be the last ones to admit that their problem is spiritual stagnation. They claim to know it all in telling us endless stories of why we should follow them and learn the

Word of God. For centuries people were forced and frightened into submission to believe or otherwise face the dire consequences of a wrathful and jealous God. Throughout history the meek have been herded like slaves by the prophets of old, kings, and barbarian dictators; many of them have lost faith and are still clinging to their brainwashed and habitual way of life.

Socially, religion has done a great service to humanity by helping members of a community to a better life, but spiritual advancement in the way of teaching the Philosophy of Love has just not materialized. Jesus said as much when he said, "In love all things are fulfilled." Every minister must have read these holy words. Why, then, are these words ignored and not preached from the pulpit and in the schools? I ask those ministers, including their superiors, "Do they not fulfill the commandments of Christ?" It is promised that if they would, the Holy Spirit will come into them, as in John 14:15–18. Those verses, I can personally testify to all my readers, are no idle words but are of the Holy Spirit and will come to pass. Religious leaders are highly respected by all their churches and congregations and they have great influence the world over; but this demonstrates, no matter what or who you are, how important it is to ask God for more light and love. I wish to remind them that the big-business idea of preaching to a large church is indeed old-fashioned. The truth is, God does not care how popular the attractions you apply are for the growth of the church, nor does He care how many sheep you herd. However, it will be all-important how many people will be influenced by a minister to live in the Philosophy of Love. If one man lives with the commandments of love, because of it I believe the church will be blessed. Those ministers are frustrated because they cannot meet the expectations of pastoring a large church. Most likely, their frustration is caused by such pressure, but whatever the cause of that epidemic I can only advise you all to relearn the words of Jesus Christ and eventually be inspired by the Holy Spirit. A frustrated clergyman cannot inspire his own family, let alone the church congregation. He is the very person who must radiate light from within, not by the forces of worldly power, but by the Philosophy of Love. Without that strength, their dogmas will not fulfill their mission. Renewed inspiration from the Holy Spirit is essential, and the manifestation thereof is Love.

So often the truth might be concealed in your ignorance because you have bartered your soul. You have promised your church that your opinion will always be second to that of theirs. Do you know that first-hand truth comes only from the Spirit of God and that everything else is man-made and translated, much misinterpreted, and twisted? I wish to stress again that it makes no difference what religious affiliation a person has; everyone can use the spiritual mixing bowl philosophy. It will produce only goodness and love, which is needed in every person's heart in all of life and in the whole universal environment. We are talking about every aspect of life that is dependent upon the Philosophy of Love. Only by its appearance can harmony and peace ever be achieved around the world. Love up until now has been used as an opportunistic tool by the affluent of power and greed, but it has never been taught or even considered as a way of life. Jesus proclaimed it anew in as much that in love all things are fulfilled, which was His doctrine. Unfortunately, religions used those words only in their dogmas to glorify traditions, but completely ignored the introduction of such a lifestyle which, in turn, will create harmony.

Utopia for mankind is at hand if truth will prevail, and holiness is conceived as an act of love rather than man-made sacred objects for pretense's sake. This charade of holiness has deceived the world, and confusion has left a legacy of turmoil and hate the world over. It was always the perfect nourishment dictators thrived on. Is it not time for truth to surface and religion to admit that it failed the teachings of Jesus and that everything depends on love?

A new age has dawned where changes will occur. Faith in your mind must be put into action and made useful. Religions must rejuvenate to truly help mankind in the Will of God, which is, and always was, the Philosophy of Love. The spoken words and actions recorded in history are the eternal testimony given to us to learn from, to accept or reject the ideals given by the prophets and a host of countless gods of history. The time has come when resurrected souls will sift through those legacies of old and will understand how to judge and find the truth in the way of love. The New Age morality will shun, and rightfully disrespect dogmas of fear, jealousy, revenge, and the warmongering gods of old. They expended their usefulness of fear, on which they feasted for a few thousand years, and transformed this planet earth into a living hell.

No religion in this world, nor any other institution of man, has the power or mandate to determine its followers for heaven. Some preachers and deans in high places pretend to have this knowledge. They frighten their congregations with the fear of hell if they do not hearken to their dogmas and excommunicate those with different opinions. Their ruthless and inflated egos are saying that the way to heaven is through the church; such assumptions have deceived the world. The Holy Spirit is telling us that we will experience heaven according to the brightness of our human soul. No other worldly influence will penetrate the realm beyond the mortal boundaries.

The time is near when the masses of educated people interested in a better lifestyle will no longer be hoodwinked by stories of old and fantasies. People are craving for more knowledge and are open to embrace true spiritual help to bring about a better way of life as promised by Jesus. Even the old-time perception of creation as outlined in the text of religion depicts a profile of primitive thinking. The belief that everything was void and desolate, with only darkness upon the face of the deep and that the spirit of God moved upon the face of the waters, is a typical assertion of man lacking spiritual knowledge because his mental horizon in the wisdom of life is earthbound. The worldly spirit is the originator of those stories and actions, and the glorification of them has given us the never-ending harvest of famine, pestilence, and wars.

Jesus said that by their fruits ye shall know them, so if we are to believe in Him, we have to cast off the old superstitious teachings of fear. The time has come for churches to clean house if they want to influence their congregations spiritually with the Philosophy of Love. Mere social power with a large flock of sheep will solve no problems; however, the time for pruning of the spiritual tree for a sweeter harvest has arrived. All glorification of traditions are useless without an act of love for the betterment and health to humanity. Teaching through fear must disappear and thereby will open the door to the Philosophy of Love, which will then finally have its beginning.

The science of theology did not reach further than the translation of the old Scripture and failed to find a higher moral way of life. They put their concerns into the figureheads of the old drama instead of learning from their unholy way of life. Theology does not question the actual lifestyle of the early prophets and kings—they only concerned themselves in the words they claim came from their God. Would they be as generous today if a murderer proclaims, "God gave me the order to do it?" In the Scriptures they seem to ignore those acts and instead glorify the command because the mere mention of God holds them in a spell. This is the greatest hypocrisy that mankind has perpetrated upon the God of Love.

The moral standard in this world is founded on evil because we condone aggressors and yet possess a United Nations with the capability to stop such wickedness. Where are the churches during such times? Is this ugliness truly all in the plans of God? I can tell you from the Holy Spirit that there is no such plan from the God of Love, but they are all the evil perceptions from the hearts of man. Religion has failed to teach love as a lifestyle to its followers, especially to stress its importance to the kings and rulers of nations because they, too, all follow religion. They have not done their job for the God of Love, but only lavished toward the god of mammon.

The time has arrived when enlightened people will finally see the falsehood of the pretense of holiness in the so-called houses of God. I hold them responsible for the miseries of this world; with their power and influence, they alone could have brought the godly lifestyle of the Philosophy of Love. They need to read over and over the teachings of Jesus starting with the verse of Saint Matthew 21:22: "And all things whatsoever ye shall ask in prayer will come unto them to teach them of all things." This challenge should be taken up by every Christian, especially by the ministry, because without those experiences, they are missing the spark of life.

The Word of God as taught by Jesus is not the sole property of any religion, but belongs to all of humanity, whosoever can or will receive it. However, the teachings have been ravished and distorted ever since their inception, and continue to be so. Big-time TV evangelism is organized by ingenious groups; their messages are designed to please mammon because they do not teach the Philosophy of Love.

Their tactics are meant to stun the unwary with confusion and to soften the heart of your pocketbook. How many TV evangelists have been exposed by the courts for fraud, or worse, but they are still being listened to from the pulpits. Some new faces continue to teach the same messages for the same hope of getting rich. Therefore, let your heart decide by using the spiritual mixing bowl, and then give your cheque instead to the needy of the world as suggested by Jesus.

Created Souls Are Not God

A raindrop is in the likeness of the sea
(Both contain water)
As the soul of man is in the likeness of God.
(Both are of the same spirit)
But in itself a drop of water can never be the sea,
Likewise, nor can man ever be God.
"Fools, what ye perceived to be God
is only His handiwork!"

4

The Teachings of Jesus

I truly believe that the aim and purpose of Jesus was not to create another church but to bring to the heart of man the true word of God, namely the Philosophy of Love. "Love thy fellow man as thyself" tells it all. It was not meant to be just a compassionate tolerance but to be lived as a way of life. If it were not so, then His whole mission would have been a mere paradox, similar to religion. They thrive on stories of the flesh but fail to bring forth the spirit of His teachings, which is to live in the Philosophy of Love. I also believe that no one can call himself or herself a Christian without following that lifestyle and therefore does not follow the Will of God without it. Remember the words of Jesus in Matthew 7:22–24 when He said, "Many will say to me in that day, Lord, Lord, have we not prophesied in thy name? and in thy name have cast out devils? and in thy name done many wonderful works? And then will I profess unto them, I never knew you: depart from me, ye that work iniquity."

This foregoing statement tells us very clearly that accepting Jesus, and even preaching in His name, is not sufficient without living the Philosophy of Love, which spells, "I am the way." There is absolutely no higher ideal, and no greater purpose for a living soul, than to master love toward all. He was hoping that after His death His teaching would continue to grow and that His Word was the beginning, and not the end, as we are to believe. He frequently stressed the importance of searching for more light and more love.

In John 14, it is very obvious that even His close disciples were often confused and did not always fully understand the meaning He conveyed. For example, in verses 5–8, it states: "Thomas saith unto Him, Lord, we know not whither thou goest; and how can we know the way? Jesus saith unto him, I am the way, the truth and the life: no man cometh unto my Father, but by me. If ye had known me, ye should have known my Father also: and from henceforth ye know Him, and have seen Him." And then in verse 9, Jesus said unto them, "Have I been so long time with you, and yet hast thou not known me, Philip? he that hath seen me hath seen the father; and how sayeth thou then, shew us the Father?"

This problem of misunderstanding and misinterpretation of His way of expression is extended into most of the believers to this very day. We do not know of the problems the early translators had nor are we aware of the true motives of those who again translated those Scriptures in the Holy Bible and other writings. Just recently it was rewritten again with changes made in the paraphrased "Living Bible." The rewriting was done to make it easier to understand, people claim, but in doing so, subtle meanings and wordings were changed from the old expressions. How often can a word or a sentence stand transfiguration and not lose its true glitter?

The Old Testament describes to us the beliefs and history of the nomadic Hebrew tribes in the Arabian region. On the other hand, the New Testament is the disciples' recollection of their master, Jesus Christ, describing His mission of bringing the Word of God. Jesus sincerely believed in the universal laws of God, thereby rightfully proclaiming that He and the Father are one. John 14:10 states that "believest thou not that I am in the Father, and the Father in me? the words that I speak unto you I speak not of myself: but the Father that dwelleth in me, he doeth the works."

This verse is a clear description, firstly that the Father He is speaking of is the Holy Spirit within and second, that He is not considering Himself an equal but rather the receiver of messages. He never professed to be God Himself—only mankind after Him has done so. In verse 12, He says, "Verily, verily, I say unto you, He that believeth on me, the works that I do shall he do also; and greater works than these shall he do: because I go unto my Father." He emphasized that greater works are in store, so that should tell us that new inspirations are still in the offing, the teachings having not been completed.

Then He continues to tell us how much knowledge of continuance can be achieved in verses 21 and 26: "He that hath my commandments, and keepeth them, he it is that loveth me: and he that loveth me shall be loved of my Father, and I will love him, and manifest myself to him. . . . But the Comforter, which is the Holy Ghost, whom the Father will send in my name, he shall teach you all things, and bring all things to your remembrance, whatsoever I have said unto you."

This foregoing verse encourages us to find the truth from within, and by such inspirations find the rightful meaning of His teaching. Jesus became inspired by asking for more light and love, and His success is demonstrated by His inspired doctrine of universal laws and mastery thereof. "Ask and it shall be given, knock and it shall be opened unto you" was a proven principle to Him because of His great desire to know. God opened the Book of Life in His soul, thereby answering all His questions from the sensual universe to the extreme mysteries beyond.

When I came across the words, "Seek and ye shall find," it was to the liking of my heart. Here was a promise and a way of proving to myself of the true existence of the God of Love. My desire to know was strong; my questions to Him were endless and some very bizarre, so it came to pass that I started to ask of His existence and so on. Prayers for more light and love became my daily communication. As the days and years passed by, inspirations of first-hand knowledge became part of me, clarifying many great mysteries about life. I am happy to mention that I received profound communication with the God of Love.

Many times I had exhilarating and uplifting experiences with the feeling of overflowing bliss. It is wonderful to know in one's heart that an answer just received came from the Holy Spirit, the only source of truth. No matter what you read, it was written by man, translated, selected and much misunderstood. Books are great—we all know that without them we would have no history and no recollection of man's past. What I am trying to say is truth is not something you read or hear, but has to be rediscovered through our soul.

The hunger for power and dominance was dictated to the body and soul of man by unscrupulous fanatics, what to believe and what is true, only to deceive the very elect. Misunderstandings abound, and I urge all you who are true of heart to ask God Himself for all finalities. He will not fail you, I can testify to that. I feel great that my ever-increasing knowledge is available just for the sake of asking. I am no special person and not without blemish; therefore I know the door will open to anyone who has the courage to knock. Those profound principles that Jesus taught are not mere idle promises but are words written in the laws of Heaven and will not fail anyone willing to receive truth. It says: "Seek and ye shall find." It does not state: "Read and believe, or listen and do not question!" Adapt to the spiritual mixing bowl; it will guide you toward the Philosophy of Love and to a new and ultimate goal for humanity.

Only through love can we reach that path to be reborn of the spirit and the flesh. It is said, "Be ye perfect as the Father which is in heaven." Our goal must be to achieve harmony in ourselves and with our fellowman. Consider the motto, "All for one and one for all." To the "God of Love," all humans are equal regardless of color and status, and the only difference appears in the knowledge of love. No other measurement can enhance your spiritual soul.

I, too, have been raised under the rules of a religion. Its surroundings are peaceful and helpful, and feel like a continuous trip on a boat gliding through life. Nondemanding, accepting in full faith the direction of the captain, but being totally ignorant of his chart. As long as you do not rock the boat, you shall sail peacefully through once again, to the uncertain yonder. This has been repeated for thousands of years. My soul was not at peace, so I rocked the boat when my mind demanded to see the chart of the captain. I desired to know the whole journey, my living soul shall not rest until the mystery of the chart is proven to me, and with that knowledge will be enlightened to follow directions and find the purpose of my destiny.

No recorded history or organization of man possessed the divinity of truth, but only the Holy Spirit through our soul can enlighten us to this glory. Jesus said many will come in my name and proclaim He is here or over there, but pay no attention, go your way and pray in silence, and then God will reward you openly. What He is telling us is to use the mixing bowl to recapture our free will and to seek the final truth always from within.

The religious jungle of man is growing by leaps and bounds: statistics show that three thousand new cults have risen since the 1960s. Many of them are founded from Bible clubs and splinter groups of religion. Just around the corner lurks deception. We are free to join anything, but we must be wary at all times. Should any one of you be looking for the God of Love, go into your chamber and pray to God directly. Ask Him for guidance in earnest, desire more light and love, and pray for peace in the world. Your efforts then shall not be in vain; it worked for me and it will work for you. This is written in the laws of heaven that those things will come to pass.

All the actions of Jesus during His lifetime, such as healing, freeing the possessed, teaching, as well as His wanderings and miracles, prophecies, and finally His death by crucifixion and resurrection, were all important to His plans. Those were the necessary tools and needs for Him to accomplish and bring across the message He lived for, the Philosophy of Love. The teaching of Love was the purpose of His life. He did not come to build a church of worldly appearance but rather the spiritual understanding and following of the Father's Will, which was love and His Church.

"Upon this rock I shall build my church"—He often used important unrelated words to stress a point. That rock He spoke of was meant to be the solid truth in the Philosophy of Love, and the Church signified His total commitment. That is the only Will God has for mankind, and all of it is to our advantage.

Jesus used this rock comparison in other verses, such as in Matthew 7:24: "Therefore whosoever heareth these sayings of mine, and does them, I will liken him into a wise man, which built his house upon a rock." He is saying that those who practice His teaching are wise and are aware of the Holy Spirit. The previous verse had a similar meaning: He spoke to church elders and followers whose life commitment was the Church. He could not express himself more forcefully in front of them than to compare His sincere performance with that of their church, and the rock being the so-called Word of God.

We find many messages of His are confounded and fit the egos of those responsible in theology. If my statements clash with your assumptions, then I will challenge any one of you in disagreement to follow His teachings. Take note of His promise that the Comforter will recall into you His spoken words. My statements, therefore, in this book are not my vague worldly opinions, but were impressed upon me by His Comforter. Christian teachings and actions have disgraced His seat in heaven. He can hear their voices raised to the glory of mammon and pretense, but they have forsaken His teachings of Love. The clouded mind of man has not even perceived of a satisfactory administrative system for our courts, politics, religion, and economy. The world is very much in need of changes to improve the above and thereby render a higher morality standard, which can all be achieved in applying the spiritual mixing bowl and living in the divine Philosophy of Love. There are no other plans and commandments that God has laid out for us; the fulfillment of Love will be our blessings.

Those with the ambitions to get rich can still do so by the way of righteousness rather than by unscrupulous greed and abusement of others. The poor will be more accessible, distribution of food can be regulated because foreign aid will not go into a dictator's bank account but instead will find its way honestly to the people in need. Military will be needed for a long time yet in order to rehabilitate aggressive countries until the message of the "Philosophy of Love" has been implemented by the United Nations of the world.

Religions should be asking themselves the question, "How do we stand spiritually in front of God?" This can quite easily be answered for those who possess honesty because spirituality is measured in terms of Love, and according to that quality, the ego will shine. There can be no mistake that the brightness of your soul represents the Book of Life. That is the answer to how everyone stands spiritually in front of God and whether you achieved in your present life eternity.

Jesus taught those laws: "Ask and it shall be given unto you. When I am gone into the Father the spirit of the Holy Ghost shall look after and inspire those who seek me or my Father."

He was not talking about His body Jesus but was referring to the teachings of the universal laws and Christ consciousness, the highest order of man's spirituality. He spoke all the parables in earthly expressions, hoping that the multitude following Him would find the heavenly meanings. He was a true prophet of self-mastery, with the laws of the universe and the Holy Spirit shining through His soul.

The Temple of God

Jesus said, "Know ye not that ye are the temple of God, and that the Spirit of God dwelleth in you? For the temple of God is holy, which temple ye are" (1 Cor. 3:16–17). And "Seek ye first the kingdom of God, and his righteousness; and all things shall be added unto you" (resurrection of your soul, through love) (Matt. 6:33).

Love

Matthew 22:37–40 states that on love hang all the laws and the prophets, the Philosophy of Love. And Luke 7:47: Sins are forgiven according to love, the Philosophy of Love.

5

Is the Church and God above Reproach?

We have been told by the ministry of the churches that God and the Church are above reproach and cannot be questioned by followers. It must be the conclusion reached by the wise men of theology. It is very surprising to me because it is in direct contradiction with the New Testament. We are reminded by Jesus to ask, and He promised us that we would receive. He went much further when He was quoted in John 14:14–18: "Ask anything in my name—I will do it—and the spirit of truth will abide with you." Then He said in verse 26, "The Comforter which is the Holy Ghost will teach you all things." The big question now is who do we believe; the rules of the churches not to question and only to believe, or shall we take the Word of Jesus who was inspired by the Holy Ghost and who encouraged us to question and to ask anything?

For me the choice is very easy to make. Forty years ago I launched my search to find the God of Love when my questions were endless, but lo and behold, the answers were like flashes of miracles to my searching, living soul. I often experienced the spiritual meaning when He stated, "Ye shall be filled to overflowing" (Matthew 7:7–8). Those two verses inspired and brought me onto the path toward truth and revealed for me God's spirit within. His words were not only said to fashion colorful sermons for the pulpit but are, in fact, the very principles from the laws of God. I wish to remind everyone that they will come to pass for those who desire to know, and that nothing will be withheld from them. With joy in my heart, I can attest to its truth because of my personal experiences of first-hand knowledge through God's communication channel of the Holy Spirit.

There is not one living soul upon this earth today who cannot be inspired by the Holy Spirit. Anyone using the simple method of the spiritual mixing bowl is launching himself or herself onto the path toward the Philosophy of Love, which is the lifestyle for mankind, glorified by the God of Love. It encompasses all commandments God ever made and highlights all the teachings of Jesus: "On their fruit ye shall know them," He said.

Mysteries between God and the living soul are manmade. Those barriers were erected by the founders of religion to exalt themselves and to have better and quicker control over their flock of sheep. Moses was a prime example because he was the only one who knew and conversed with his God whose every commandment he endeavored to fulfill. When Moses made war on the weak, he blamed the command of God to kill all, including women and children, and to save only the gold. I wish to repeat some of Moses's deeds, because I don't consider them acts of love and certainly not of the Holy Spirit. He blamed God for those commands!

History repeated itself again and again, and even in our day, every calamity that strikes man is blamed as an act of God. Some renowned prophets of old who claimed to have communicated with God, as strange as it seemed, most often turned out to be killers—Elijah slew 450 prophets of Baal. Today such actions are described as mass murders. Jehovah killed all the first-born childern of Egypt; he was the Lord Himself and the God of Moses. I cannot help but refer again to the words of Jesus who said, "Ye shall know them by their fruits." The greatest mystery in reading the old Scriptures is, of course, the blunt evil committed by the gods of the times, because generations of people are molding their religion according to the examples of those warrior gods.

Since the time of Jesus, religion has interwoven His teachings with the Old Testament and has arrived on a God of duality of good and evil. Religions claim He is a jealous God and we must love Him or be destroyed; He is one who will send pestilence with the blink of an eye. On Judgement Day, one will be given everlasting life and the other will be burnt forever in hell, and in spite of all His wickedness, they still claim He is all love. Such a God of good and evil has been confusing to seekers and has turned away generations of people looking instead for a God of Love.

If the gods of the times were true and not man-made, I would not be here writing about the Philosophy of Love. There would be no such thing as a God of Love because evil and love do not mix: Jesus said we cannot serve God and mammon alike. The one we call the Creator of all things has been disfigured, shamed in breaking all commandments, called a jealous and vindictive God, and portrayed as a warmonger and killer by those God-makers.

I also find it worthwhile to mention that one of the world's greatest evils around the globe is that God and Jesus are being used as a collection box: while millions die in hunger, shamelessly preachers extort ten percent of all earnings in His name, plus they devour widows' houses to keep their luxury in splendor. Wars have never ceased to be because religion has failed to teach the Philosophy of Love; ministers' sermons are full of blame to others and have not given any light to darkness. The secret chambers they are hiding behind will one day be exposed as empty because true seekers will begin to ask God themselves and will be inspired from within. The autocracy and infallible opinions are just not compatible with love and are too complicated for people to understand.

The true laws of God, which revolve around love, are simple, straightforward, and should be understood by all living souls. The Philosophy of Love, which derives from the spirit of the Creator, has no hidden secrets and no forbidden tree for anyone to become entangled in. All those false teachings about God have been man-created and must be undone by man. For thousands of years, the man-made war lords were the conception of false prophets. It is not easy to sort out the religious maze created by man in the name of mammon because they flourished to golden temples, the ultimate in man-made glory.

I have been told from within that the glory of God is love, likewise sacred and holy places, where love is practiced and taught. No other deserves to be called holy because it is the commandment and the Will of the God of Love. If religion does not teach us how to live love, then its members are not Christians, neither do they know the God of Love. Every person must find out for himself by taking a look at the scale of good and evil and to practice using the spiritual mixing bowl. It is never too late to walk and be guided onto the path of goodness and justice on the way to repentance and overcoming the evils of this world.

Truth

How mysterious the meaning behind Truth.
What does it convey in our minds and hearts?
We read a script or poem and are taught about it—
Even commanded to believe, accept and not to question.
How can we allow our intelligence to be trampled on this
    way?

Without questions man would be but a mere parrot in a
  cage—
Therefore question the principle and word called Truth.
Do not let yourself be troubled into a confused state—
But place those thoughts into the spiritual mixing bowl
And allow your soul to take over its care.
For your desire to know and constant search,
As day follows night, it will come forth again.
Not in its state to be questioned ever,
Behold! In its "brightness" you will know the Truth.

There is only one source where Truth can be verified, and
that sanctified shrine is within us. Remember the breath of
life given to us at the time of birth? I call it the spiritual soul.

Jesus said, "Even the spirit of Truth, whom the world
cannot receive, because it sees him not neither knoweth him:
but ye know him; for He dwelleth with you, and shall be in
you forever. Keep my commandments, which are of the
Father that sent me." This passage from John 14:15–24 ties in
with the Philosophy of Love.

6

Holy Pretence

All around the world, we see more freedom, openness, and freer speech, thus giving us more courage to open the door of astonishments. Never before has dirty laundry been brought out of the closet of tormented souls. The women's liberation movements and the equal rights amendments are in the beginning stages of important debates, which eventually will create equality between women and men. It is evident that people in businesses, politics, religion, and the population in general are beginning to change their ways regarding morality and equality. In business, women are demanding no gender discrimination, equal pay for equal work and no sexual harassment, which is considered a crime. Take note: harassment is no longer permitted in a civilized country regardless of whether you are the boss, a politician, a law man, a minister or however famous or renowned you are. Such degradation is shameful in a civilized society and has to be aired to make people aware that many who are relied upon have abused their high positions and trust.

During the past few years, we have been reading endless headlines of sexual assaults in the confines of religion. Dozens of priests have been charged with such offenses—these are people who have sworn allegiance to God to work in His name. Such incidents are far from isolated but are widespread the world over. Is it possible that man-made false teachings of God have run full circle and are gradually expanding? I feel strongly that those pretentious holy men are lacking spiritual inspiration and are resorting to the worldly pleasures instead. We will see more and more of such erosion because an educated population will be demanding teachings of substance of a God they can live with and trust in, and He in them. Make no bones about it, holy pretence is coming to an end, but holy actions will be the future of the world if we heed the call. Religious crusades have stirred the world with powerful words and promises; they are heralding with trumpets! Accept Jesus in your heart now and all sins shall be forgiven—this simplistic statement is not true because sins are not forgiven until the due process of love has compensated for them.

Luke 7:47 states: "Wherefore I say unto thee, Her sins, which are many, are forgiven; for she loved much: but to whom little is forgiven, the same loveth little." In the above example, Jesus is telling us that compensation and redemption for sins begins with love. Those preachers have learned the Bible in a very short time but missed out much of the meaning of the teachings. They never fail to remind you that whatever you give in gold in the name of Jesus, you shall receive back tenfold. This statement, as well, is not of Jesus. This is a monetary trap, and it does not come true because it serves only mammon. This willful deception is not honest because the parable was meant in the context of the spiritual value, in love. Knowing human nature, those two foregoing promises are the trump cards to win over the people's hearts; or was it for repentance's sake? No point in guessing, actions speak many times louder than words. Remember Jesus telling us that stars will be falling from heaven? Well, the time has arrived because many of the superstar TV preachers, who were bright stars to many, have fallen from the highest realm of man's heaven to the lowest level on earth. I do not have to tell you why, but, rather, I will let Jesus confirm the reason.

In Mark 12:38–40, He states, "Those which devour widows' houses shall receive greater damnation."

Jesus encouraged His disciples to carry just one coat and no further provisions because He maintained the believers would take care of them. "Sufficient into the day is the evil thereof" was another warning of His. He told the rich man to sell all he had, give it to the poor, and follow Him. Why did He not demand to bring his money to the church, as all ministers are doing today? Why did Jesus not ask His disciples to collect 10 percent of income from all their followers? Today all ministers preach it. Jesus told the rich man to share his wealth with the poor, but He did not demand of him one farthing to help support His ministry. . . It seems obvious that the 10-percent demand must be a hangover from the time of Moses because during his time, it was demanded that a certain amount of war bounties be put into the treasury of God. This was a command by the Lord. What is disturbing about this treasury is the fact that all those riches came directly from the innocent victims slaughtered by greed-obsessed barbarian tribes.

I can assure you from my heart that the God of Love I speak of had nothing to do with the treasury of the Lord; it smells very much of Satan rather than of love. Many high-powered superstar preachers are believing that the millions they harvest in gold are their reward from God for spreading His Word. They are lavishing this glory upon themselves and are not ashamed to live in luxury amongst impoverished neighborhoods. They tell you to give all you can to their church because you can expect this tenfold deal from God! Many widows have lost their homes because of this inhumanely conceived trickery. I believe in the upkeep and all the expenses of their church being provided for, but all the surplus should be taxed or distributed to the hungry and the suffering in the world. Any church conducting other businesses and that has hidden savings to safeguard for a rainy day is not following His teachings. According to Jesus, "Sufficient unto the day is the evil thereof."

For thousands of years, religion has been competing for more elaborate buildings and golden symbols to impress the God of their choice. Because of it, they hope one day to be rewarded to sit in the realm of their God. Remember the golden temple of Solomon? It is written that God was pleased, but we must also remember that the people who were overtaxed had to war against other kingdoms for their gold, land, and slaves. The temple of Solomon was not built with love but by hardships and slave labor; therefore, it had nothing to do with the God of Love but had everything to do with the glory of man. Spiritual inspiration is urging me to tell the churches of this world that it is not the glitter of gold and riches of displays in your church, but only the teachings and actions of love that will make it holy.

Humanity of the New Age is anxiously searching for a God here and now, a God in whom they can find the light of Truth and inspiration. They will no longer be content with ancient dogmas and false prophets with their bloated egos full of useless traditions. Their ways have no power to reverse the world's trend of self-destruction. I am told that the only alternative to peace and prosperity is in the Philosophy of Love.

7

In the Image of God

The solar system and elements were always the inspiring powers and the pictures of greatness and glory upon all life. On this complex and wonderful planet Earth, our accumulated knowledge of science is probing evermore into the recesses of nature above and below. People are trying to find and explore all there is, and what influences every fibre in our physical bodies. We have cultivated the soil, fished the seas, flown in the air, and have tested the weightlessness of outer space, but in spite of all these accomplishments, we have not yet reached the end of knowledge, only the beginning!

The diversity of nature has surely confused our senses in judging material objects of spiritual and divine values. Ever since ancient times, mankind was able to observe and feel the influences of life and started to react upon them. Our sensual mind comprehended only the worldly spirit forces and feasted on all excesses from our sensual thought accumulation. This spirit has been applied by us to reach our worldly goals faster in our earthly cycle without the influence of the soul, its priority being the pleasures of the flesh. Power and greed know no boundaries in its wake, nor is there a shortage to influence the worldly powerful to images they made god.

The worldly gods of the times ranged from the favorite sun, moon, stars, birds of many feathers, the spirits of all the elements, animals of various kinds and then, of course, the great gods, man himself. The movement of the sun during the day, and then the appearance of the moon at night were interpreted as day and night, and this reasoning was the beginning of astrology. In all four corners of this world, the godly glorification of those heavenly bodies has endured for thousands of years in the history of mankind. The ancestral tree of the gods started with the sun and spread into different branches of gods as time passed by. The glory finally settled upon the kings and pharaohs because the seers and prophets interpreted the horoscopes in their favor as being the reincarnation of the supreme God (which, or course, has always been the sun god). All the above systems of gods up until now were strictly man-made apparitions and idols of the worldly spirit.

The dust of the earth of which man is composed, how could it possibly be in the image of God, regardless of which shape or form? It is generally believed that God is expressing Himself in the Holy Spirit and therefore is not composed of any kind of created material. If this is a reasonable assumption, then the image can only be referred to when we are believing that mankind possesses a spiritual soul. If the soul is not in use, then we can state with certainty that there is no image for comparison.

What is left standing is a creature of pretense: it knows the needs but ignores them, talks of love but does not practice it, believes in God but does not know Him. The prophets or messiahs of religion have renewed or changed the thinking and worshiping of their followers with their newly inspired messages of the last few thousand years. They were drastic changes from the old-time religion, but gradually down the centuries, they were incorporated into the doctrines of to-day's religions.

Until the Middle Ages, very few people were awakened

through the influence of their spiritual soul to overcome the worldly spirit of its evil influences. Those who did so are marked in history; they not only preached but also tried to live their lives in the virtues of love. Some of the prophets or messiahs who influenced old-time religions and new ones were: Jesus, Buddha, Muhammad, Krishna, Zoroaster, etc., and in the faraway Americas, there were the old-time renowned Quetzalcoatl, etc.

Their messages and doctrines greatly influenced the churches of old as well as new religions around the world. I am also aware that their teachings have at some time suffered through purges and changes by emperors and church elders in the path of changing history. The Bible is a great example of reversion, with its constant rewriting into different versions and glossing over phrases that they insist are the crude expressions of old. Those changes are diluting the meaning and the spirit in which the messages were conveyed.

Is it any wonder that a religion such as Christianity can splinter into hundreds of different denominations because each one thinks it has found a missing link of truth? It is unfortunate that the Christian churches are not founded upon the fundamental principle of the doctrine of Jesus, that in love all things are fulfilled. If we accept that as a true statement, then it should be so that every Christian will try and live in the Philosophy of Love. In doing so, we will resurrect our spiritual soul to its rightful place, be influenced by it knowingly and continuously, and bring about harmony between body and soul.

The significance of the Holy Spirit is to inspire us so that we can strengthen our constitution of Love, and in that lifestyle avoid evil. This is the ageless message from the true God of Creation that I call the God of Love. In our confusion of what constitutes the true God between all of the choices mankind has made in the past ages, it follows that we must direct our vision toward creation. The name of Creator was bestowed upon all gods in the past and was not contested because there are no boundaries for the human brain to comprehend.

We have an arguable position for the god phenomena since most religions and believers in this world attest that the Supreme Being is divine and is, in essence, the Holy Spirit, permeating all of creation and being everywhere. If, then, we accept and understand spirituality on those terms, we begin to realize that this Comforter is not an individuality that can, or will, reincarnate in the form of a person from time to time, as imagined and written. Those reincarnated gods confound reality (it would be similar if we harness a bottle of air and call it the Powerful Element that caused the dreadful tornado or hurricane).

I have been told that this does not happen and that the Holy Spirit has never been divided, personified or materialized in any shape or form for man's sake. In the laws of creation, the Holy Spirit is with us, but our free will must desire this communication come about because no other medium can bring this birthright into our soul. Jesus tells us in His teachings of so many different ways that we can become inspired and to live thereafter. Jesus is an excellent example for us regarding the Holy Spirit because He described it with various names, but referred to the same meaning. When He was baptized by John, it was said that the Holy Ghost descended upon Him, and because of it, He was bestowed the title of Christ. From then on, followers called it the Christ Spirit. In some instances He referred to it as the Comforter, coming into you if you follow His doctrine. His favorite expression of all was the reference to His Father, "Which is in Him." He said that is why people believe it meant He is equal to God.

However, this cannot be correct because He stated, "My

Father in me is doing the works." In John 14:10, he says, "Believest thou not that I am in the Father, and the Father in me? The words that I speak unto you I speak not of myself; but the Father that dwelleth in me, He doeth the works." This verse is telling us that the Holy Spirit abided in Him and is inspiring Him in what to say and what He should do. There is absolutely no illusion that the Holy Spirit was inspiring Him; the description made it clear and does not in any way create a confusion of the wordings. Throughout His teachings recorded in the Bible, He went to extreme length to repeat often that of Himself He can do nothing, and He gave all the credit of His knowledge and His doings to the Holy Spirit of God. No matter how great Jesus was, and how much we glorify Him for His works, honoring Him is highly commendable and respectful. We must also be reminded that there are no incarnate man gods and never were, this wishful thinking bears no fruit. Although the imposter gods stole the glitter, there was always the True creator of Creation, the Holy Spirit (God of Love).

Jesus is an excellent example of how an enlightened living soul is declared to be God by His followers because such greatness had never been seen before. We must take His Word to heart when He boldly reminded us that we can do likewise, and that even greater things are possible than He has done. To me, that surprising statement contains a plea for continuation of His mission, which in summary reveals the Philosophy of Love. When Christianity is sprouting its seeds and the buds are forming, the resurrected soul must then be realized and guide us into a harmonious existence between body and soul, to regain once more the respect between man and nature. Pollution is the silent killer of life and its food chain; there must be a new commandment heading the list of the ten, "Thou shalt not pollute," because by its neglect all the others are broken. Likewise, if you are a saint by virtue of the Ten Commandments and ignore the pollution of the universe, you have become a sinner in breach of creation.

Orthodox religions have their dogmas and traditions written in stone. Upon inauguration of an accepted belief, they were made canon law, and after that were never ever to be changed. Wrinkles and injustice are riddling many of their teachings and are gradually surfacing even more as humanity progresses along the path of democracy, freedom, and equality. Failings in their doctrines to uphold the equality of all people regardless of race or gender of the sexes, and between rich and poor is the number one demand of the New World democracy system.

The light must be shining brightly toward the above goals; therefore, the tempest stone (fanaticism) with its inscriptions will not last into all eternity because the worldly spirit must, and will, change according to universal laws on which human morality and existence depend. Renewal is the law of Heaven and of Earth. Man cannot stop and hinder a righteous path forever without meeting dire consequences along the way. Its darkened soul has forced mankind for thousands of years to live blindly, to repent and sin, and sin and repent, but has failed to convey the embracing Light of Love for mankind's salvation. The first commandment of democracy and freedom must be equality. Ask yourself, "Has my religion lived up to this?" Equal rights for men and women is the beginning, and this must be enshrined, accepted, and preached from all pulpits and educational systems.

No one owns another person, but everyone has the privilege to raise, befriend, and love one another. Distinction between rich and poor is outrageous because we all need one another; therefore, let no one build a caste system between people. Color and race is a destined privilege to each person, no matter what outward appearance one has. Remember, we were told by Jesus that in His Father's house there are many mansions. Here on this earth, we are combined, and have a purpose of mission to accept, understand, and show tolerance and love toward all of Creation, especially toward your own kind. Below the skin we are flesh and blood with a functional body and hopefully, an active spiritual soul. The aura of an active or inactive soul is far more discriminative and appalling between the races than the appearance of color will ever be.

If you look into history, there was rarely a war caused because of color, but throughout the memory of man, they were fought in the name of religion. In extreme fanaticism they were termed the "holy wars," and the instigators of them were usually the combination of being the political and spiritual leaders of the country. Such total dictatorships are the agents of havoc, endlessly using their god for unconditional commitments of the people. From here on, a brainwashed and enslaved populace will obey all the commands of their man-god, and no matter how bizarre or wicked they may be, such mental slavery is the foundation behind the holy war.

Many such examples can be witnessed, even today, in many lands, whereas ordinary dictatorship is strictly political, using military force and oftentimes against their own people. The above mentioned leaderships are the kings of darkness, the abusers of the worldly spirit and the instigators of terror. We of the countries called the free world have risen to the surface of darkness, swimming in the current of remorse, but by lifting our heads, we will finally see the light. Pray for light and more love to resurrect your soul from the darkness of hell, because it is your birthright to live in the knowledge of the Holy Spirit. I am urging everyone to use the spiritual mixing bowl. By doing so, we will rise to the knowledge of love and the path of salvation. By this means, our accursed deviation of the soul can be compensated as prophesied by Jesus, but restitution will be demanded to the last farthing.

Those were the spoken words of the Master Himself, and they definitely align with the law of compensation. We will also have to bear the principle of harvest: "We will reap as we have sown." Like it or not, it will come to pass. Sure, false prophets proclaim otherwise; they blow the horn that all sins are forgiven by the simple declaration, "I love Jesus," but Jesus never meant it in that manner. Those are again twisted words!

Why did He stress again, and throughout His teaching, to follow and fulfill His doctrine? He complained that they professed to love Him but ignore His commandments. He stressed that they must endeavor to be doers of the Word and not only listeners. I remind all Christians to read His teachings again, because they seem to glorify many shadows and ignore the cause of the shining light. The worldly spirit is flattering their egos. They read the parables and feast on their earthly dialogue, only to miss out on its heavenly meaning. There are so many examples in today's Christian teachings that are not true.

The age is near where more and more seekers of the God of Love will find Truth from within, rather than only as envisioned by the rulers and interpreters of theology. I fully agree that religious teachings should not interfere with politics and schooling, but the true Word of the Holy Spirit which is manifested in the Philosophy of Love, should be heralded and taught everywhere throughout the world because it is neither political nor religious. Love is the number-one commandment on this earth and throughout the mansions of the heavens. Until humankind will adjust to these laws of the Holy Spirit, the miracles of peace cannot, and will not, be manifested amongst the living souls on this planet. Those above words are not derived from wild speculation, nor are they imaginary of the worldly spirit. Those words are not mine but are the will of the Holy Spirit. There is no cause for me to carry mischievous intentions in my heart to influence anyone against their present belief, but my soul is telling me that this new Philosophy will put a halo around those who will embrace it and are living this new way of Life.

So many people out there call themselves atheists, but I have found that many of them have read the Old Testament or heard about it. To their horror, they cannot accept gods who gave orders to kill innocent people again and again, and they rightfully question, "Where is God in wars, and whenever tragedy strikes?" Millions today die of hunger around the world, and so atheists' arguments definitely have a valid point, especially when religion proclaims that it all belongs to the plan of God and offers no other explanation. However, the Holy Spirit tells me that the plan of God was established in the beginning of all Creation and perfected in principles and laws that take care of things into eternity.

I believe to this day that the old Scriptures are read in absentia of mind; they are not focused on the reality that existed at that time. It doesn't seem to matter if a prophet or a renowned biblical figurehead committed murder or caused a holocaust of a whole people like Jericho. It seems to be acceptable to religion that such horrible atrocities were the will and command of God. At the same time, religion claims love and justice of that God. How warped can the acceptability of the worldly spirit be? There are absolutely no boundaries of morality in man's mind when he perceives a shadow he fears as God. Fright of this unknown abomination is the direct result for the mass hysteria of a people to follow the powerful. They believe he may be a chosen one of the mysterious spirit that is loaded with mischief for those who do not hearken.

71

Jesus said, "Follow me and do my will, and the Holy Ghost will be with you, teaching you of all things." If you are one of the fortunate people who believes in His teachings, then you are probably experiencing the Holy Ghost, which surely is the greatest experience man can perceive. Why, then, do you need to see a walking mass of flesh in front of you resembling whoever, or whatever shape or form? The mortal body of Jesus, Buddha, or any other messenger of God, is not as great as the teachings they brought to us.

Jesus said that "many times of myself I can do nothing, the Word is from my Father which is in Heaven." His way of teaching confused many. Even the most important metaphor, "I and my Father are one" means nothing more than that He is in harmony, totally devoted to and completely understanding the Word of God and the universal laws. He did not compare Himself with God—that is a misconception of His followers because He was much too humble to display such arrogance. Only worldly people do Him this injustice. Spiritually inspired souls like His have no need to impress the skeptics because their kingdom is not of this world. His mission was for us to follow Him, meaning His teachings and not His body. His ambition was to point the way so that mankind would learn to live in the Philosophy of Love, no more or no less.

What has happened since the departure of those mighty men who spent their lives over the great cause of Love? Now we find that nobody really teaches their doctrine of how to live, love as a family, and conduct business and politics. These doctrines are the ultimate and the Will of God. What we find instead is that churches all over the world are full of tradition, added and revised tradition, and more and more tradition! They are busy renovating their golden temples to impress the Second Coming of Jesus whom, they insist, will come to reign, ignoring His true mission, which was to inspire love in human life.

Your economy is none of His concern. In all probability you have forgotten His statement, "My kingdom is not of this world." Christianity, as practiced today, is an insult to the spirit of Christ because it relays the teachings of Christ to its own dogmas enforced by man, and not the Philosophy of Love taught by the Holy Spirit. Is your mind ravaged by man-taught assumptions, or is your heart filled with the influence of your spiritual soul? As a Christian it is your duty to put into motion the teachings of Jesus that in Love our lives will be fulfilled.

My message from the Holy Spirit is that all beliefs of this world, and of the past, must perceive a moral standard of love. The spiritual mixing bowl contains the guidelines whereby the doctrines of Christ can be fulfilled or where any other belief will find the measuring stick to resurrect their soul to the rightful place of the living.

8

My Kingdom Is Not of This World

This statement was a mystery to those people of the time two thousand years ago, and it still baffles most of us today. It has been interpreted in various ways, but I want to describe the inspirational message that came personally to me. I staunchly believe the phrase, "Ask and you shall receive" because this divine promise would share all secrets between God and man. Patience will be the only requirement because certain messages may not reach us until we are ready to understand them. I have practiced this for forty years of my life and can attest that those are not mere empty words but are true in their statement.

In most religious organizations, it is taught that God is Love; if that is true and acceptable to us, then it would be equally true that the kingdom Jesus was speaking of was the Philosophy of Love. His commandment, "Love thy fellow man as thyself," speaks for itself. All His teachings reflect respect to others, sharing, compassion, truthfulness, and justice. All are expressions from the spiritual kingdom that are a guiding light for man to live by.

The expression of Jesus, "Man does not live on bread alone," is another example that our sensual life must also have spiritual influence. That is where our soul plays its part by translating all spiritual messages to our worldly mind regardless of the quality of good or evil. When someone says that he or she had an inspiration, heard voices or messages, or experienced other apparitions, his or her soul is the medium for receiving and sending those translations that are then stored in the memory. All things pertaining to the five senses are handled by our brain and the resulting world thereof. This functional body received a soul on the first breath upon birth, which will depart from a being on its last breath.

This, of course, will draw strong criticism from those who believe man and soul to be one unit for ever, rather than a duality. Jesus said, "What would it gain a man if he conquered the whole world and lose his soul?" Jesus knew the soul was distinct; otherwise He would have most likely used the word *life* instead.

Another fine example is Elijah: he prayed to God that the departed soul of the dead child may return (1 Kings 17:21–22). Those are fine examples for those who believe in the Bible the way it was written. For my part, I am not repeating my belief because of those quotations I have read, but I became convinced only through my personal experiences.

I prayed for forty years, for more light and more love, to the God of Love and not to the gods of the times, and my cup has overflowed many times since. Now I am trying to share, in this book, my personal experiences and how I went about the search for the God of Love. The kingdom of God can only be understood if you know yourself. Those who do not understand the function of the soul will interpret God as they did for thousands of years. I call them the gods of the times because beliefs were shaped according to the seers and prophets' abilities to interpret their dreams and visions. Fear was the big drawing card during biblical times. Anyone who read the Scriptures knows that the gods had no love; they were cold-blooded warriors. That, of course, is exactly what those dictatorial rulers and kings wanted so that they could justify their own beastly behavior.

We must free our soul from those abominations and instead find the God of Love. Jesus preached how His kingdom can be attained, and it was His hope for us to follow and to continue the message of love. He said, if you believe in Him, the Holy Ghost shall enter and teach you all things. That message, too, I can testify does come true as sure as night follows day. The Comforter will teach you all things (John 14:26, 15:26, 16:13). Jesus advised us to follow His teachings, "Seek and ye shall find," meaning seek within, because the Holy Ghost is not of this world and will inspire us only through our soul. He gave us the opportunity to find ourselves and to begin realizing the connection between God and man. Jesus Himself did it that way, and all His teachings were the result of that direct spiritual communication.

Jesus proclaimed, "From myself I could do nothing, everything comes from my Father who is in Heaven." When He said, "My Father and I are one," He meant the teachings and the laws of God, which He comprehended, believed, and lived were in total harmony with His being. He also knew that all truth has not been revealed to man as yet. Jesus foresaw that His life here on earth would be shortened, and He expected us to continue His ministry. That is why He stressed in John 14:12, "Verily, verily, I say unto you, He that believeth on me, the works that I do shall he do also; and greater works than this shall he do, because I go into my Father."

This foregoing statement about greater works that can be done explains quite clearly that His teachings were not the end of all knowledge. There is, and must be, continuance of the Philosophy of Love, until mankind finds the key to live in peace in His kingdom of spiritual love and not the worldly kingdom of power and greed.

9

The Breath of Life

The law of balance between the physical and spiritual creation begins when the soul enters the human body upon the baby's first breath. Its memory of the previous spiritual existence is normally erased. I believe that only a faint recollection may hover about us at the beginning to enable us to recognize the two poles of good and evil. At an early age, we do become aware of the power within us to make choices between those two poles. This inborn feeling of the free will could be described as a subconscious image, a guiding principle to enhance love and morality into our lives.

From babyhood until the beginning of school, the child has been influenced, by its parents and others around him or her. At this tender age, a mold is forming to shape its character, and this ego will most likely be the major influence in dominating the life of this person. From here on, in the fortunate parts of the world, the educational system is taking over. Right from the beginning of grade one, the Philosophy of Love should be introduced as a subject in the curriculum of all schooling, including universities. Love is not only for families; it must extend into every business aspect, into all politics and every facet of life. It would, and should, be the number one subject for all mankind to live by and—for the first time—the laws of the land would be shared in harmony with the laws of the Creator.

Pollution would be harnessed, eliminating many diseases and hunger of this world. All evil is man-made. For whatever laws are broken, by a single living soul, perpetuated by the masses or an entire country, the consequences will never be too far behind. It is engraved in the Book of Life: "All for one and one for all," or "Ye shall reap as ye have sown." Those laws in this universe will not change.

The free will bestowed upon us in the beginning has given us, by our own choices and workings, the experiences we have at present. Our spiritual soul influence we perceive will directly determine the morality standard in politics, business or otherwise. A business transaction made with love will bring greater satisfaction for all people involved, and in return will reflect trust and goodwill from all customers. Politicians would truly work and make decisions for the good of the people and their country. They must be the jewels of the community and will enjoy and feel happy serving their community. On the other hand, self-serving arrogance on display today is giving the land bankruptcy instead of prosperity from the underhanded dictators of a society.

The cycle of evil can be broken by using the spiritual mixing bowl and applying only the sterilized thoughts and plans thereof. We owe it to ourselves to live a clean and happy life and hope that it will rub off on all those closely associated with us. How fortunate for you out there who have found, and are mastering, the balance of your body and soul. You are the angels amongst men who deserve the praise under the light of heaven. Your integrity will brighten the soul of others and bring them the joy of redemption.

The entity called the soul has once again been given another chance, through the grace of God, to shed its accumulated burdens of previous experiences here on earth. I am told that the breath of life, soul or whatever terminology you wish to use for this computer chip of spiritual "us," has returned again for a purification treatment. Life is hard to understand, and nearly impossible to live, for so many un-fortunate souls who wish to be dead rather than face another tomorrow. To appease the tormented, religion tells us that it is the "Will of God" or an "Act of His great Plan,"of which only He knows the reasons why. I am certain that the seekers of today require more substance from this explanation than those of yesteryear; we have come a long way since the days when questioning of such matters was taboo.

All religious leaders of the world seem to know, and have read in their Scripture, that prophets of old communi-cated with their God directly, and God with them. Jesus told us that He communicated with His God, and God with Him, through the Holy Ghost. Why do they not, therefore, contact God themselves to ask questions that are such mysteries to man? Is it not time for them to communicate personally with the Holy Spirit?

Matthew 7:7 states: "Ask, and it shall be given you," and in John 14:21, Jesus says, "He that has and keepeth my commandments I shall manifest myself to him." What has gone wrong since those days of contact? Is it because man has only read and learned out of books since the time of Jesus? Or has the demand of religions, that their holy opin-ions should never be challenged, overstepped the opinion of God?

The teachings of Jesus encourage us to ask, to seek within, and He vowed that nothing be withheld from us. I can personally testify that these promises are true. Opinions and dogmas are of little spiritual value if they cannot with-stand the test of Truth. No writing in this sensual world is worth its salt without the test of fair criticism. It will expose the hidden values, if any, to the masses of people, and Truth shall brighten our hearts once more.

The living soul, with all its mind and body, is wandering with the five sensual dimensions to bring about its material goal. If the right approach to spiritual awareness is taught to the living soul at a young age, the expression of love would be practiced. This will bring worldly ambitions to a harmonious outcome instead of harm by these actions. Our spiritual mixing bowl, which is always with us, can be used to bring about this balance into all our affairs. We must pray to keep our body and soul working together so that we can fulfill the divine Will to live the glory in the Philosophy of Love.

Referring to one of the phrases in the teachings of Jesus, He tells us that the purpose of life and death is Love, because all commandments and laws are fulfilled in this one word. This statement makes it clear to all of us that nothing is more important in this world than teaching and living the Philosophy of Love. There is no other vehicle to enable the flesh to master and overcome the temptations of evil in our quests, only the awakening of communications and inspirations through our spiritual soul (Matt. 13:52).

The process of redemption works through love. This is why the grace of God gives us one more chance to experience again as a "living soul" on this earth. We are told that these occurrences will happen often to our "soul being" in the spiritual realm of God, as in Job 33:27–30:

> He looketh upon men, and if any say, I have sinned, and perverted that which was right, and it profited me not;
> He will deliver his soul from going into the pit, and his life shall see the light.
> Lo, all these things worketh God often times with man,
> To bring back his soul from the pit, to be enlightened with the light of the living.

Any tainted "breath of life" that harvested the fruit of darkness in its previous life cycle will have to consider the pit of darkness. This is not a punishment from God but self-realization of shame from the beholder because riches and fame, the glory for mammon, and all harvests of evil have dimmed the light of free expression in this dimension of the soul. The pit of darkness refers to this particular celestial state. There is another mention of such places in Deuteronomy 32:34: "Is not this laid up in store with me, and sealed up among my treasures?"

My favored description of the realm of souls is expressed clearly when Jesus stated, "In my Father's house there are many mansions." This refers to spiritual places for the souls—not for mortal bodies. He also said, "I go and prepare a place for you"; this, too, is a place for immortal souls. For those who have overcome, and thereby freed their souls, He extended this invitation to be with Him. In John 14:2–3, He says, "And if I go and prepare a place for you, I will come again, and receive you unto myself; that where I am, there ye may be also."

For the Christians who do not believe in the duality of the living soul, there will be many unanswered questions in the teaching of the Christ Jesus. We all know that the time will come when our physical body will be worn out, and so-called death occurs. The body will crumble again into the earth from whence it came, and at this moment in time, our spiritual soul, or the so-called breath of life, will separate and leave the body to enter into a mansion as previously described. This concludes the purpose and the mysterious cycle of life of duality called the "living soul." Its trials and experiences in this worldly mansion of creation called Earth will always influence the future of the existing living souls. During birth, the soul of the newborn baby combines with the body as one and leaves the mortal manifestation in its last breath of life. Normally this is the end of the worldly memory, and the brain will no longer function from this moment on.

In many Christian beliefs, this is the total end for the

living soul until the physical resurrection day. They do not believe in the separate entity of a spiritual soul that leaves the body upon death. Although many references to a Spiritual Soul are mentioned by Jesus, Revelation 3:12 makes it clear to us the reward that the soul could inherit when it says, "Him that overcometh will I make a pillar in the Temple of the Lord, and he shall go no more out."

This indicates that those living souls lived in the Philosophy of Love (the Father's Will) and will stay in the realm of heaven. They, therefore, have no need for another cycle of life (to be reborn). "Hearken you that have ears but cannot hear, they have eyes but do not see, They have listened but do not understand." These words of Jesus are as much needed today as they were during His lifetime. So many important parables of His are distorted because the readers did not understand the "spiritual meaning" through the worldly story He intended to convey. Recall John 6:40,44,45,47:

> And this is the will of him that sent me, that every one which seeth the Son, and believeth on him, may have everlasting life: and I will raise him up at the last day.
>
> No man can come to me, except the Father which hath sent me draw him: and I will raise him up at the last day.
>
> It is written in the prophets, And they shall be all taught of God. Every man therefore that hath heard, and hath learned of the Father, cometh unto me.
>
> Verily, verily, I say unto you, He that believeth on me hath everlasting life.

Note also John 8:51: "Verily, verily, I say unto you, If a man keep my saying, he shall never see death." The above verses all refer to this: when believing in Him and the Philosophy of Love, not death but only everlasting life is promised. "I will raise him up the last day," He said. This means that the death and the resurrection that occur are strictly for the spiritual soul of man and not for his body. Man has put too much emphasis into his mortal being, finding difficulty in understanding that the body is only the vehicle through which to express the soul. Upon death it has served its purpose and the immortal soul continues on its journey until it reaches that harmony befitting the realm in the mansions of the souls.

The concept of raising all the dead bodies from a million years ago would lead to the assumption that the resurrection would serve no purpose to man or God. This chaotic vision of belief defies all sense of today's man, and I am told by the Holy Spirit that this barbaric teaching is the invention of religion. Such a mortal resurrection would fill the world with billions upon billions of people. According to such teachings, the wicked are cast into the everlasting fire, while the good will glory in God. It befits the teachings of those barbarous gods who commanded man to kill. It was instilled into me to consult again the mixing bowl, and any teachings that clash with any of the virtues of Love are not of the God of Love. According to my analysis, not one shred of love is involved in such mortal resurrections as imagined by religion; therefore, these are of the worldly spirit. Love must be the essence of all religious teachings before you dare to call it the Truth of the God of Love.

I never relied upon the various opinions formed by others, neither have I tried to form my own in these matters. By ringing the bells with prayer for more light and love, I was eventually inspired with clarified messages of Truth from within. It is very gratifying to know that there is actually a supernatural communication system that can influence us in so many different ways, and the methods of contact are as variable as the winds.

In my reflection of the past forty years, my longings were

not of worldly aspirations. My interest was concentrated strictly in the Philosophy of Love, and I resigned myself into this newfound hobby with great enthusiasm. I promised myself to leave no stone unturned in order to succeed in my venture. With all the sincerity in my heart, I set out on a journey to prove to myself something that the whole world is wondering about. Is there truly such a thing as the elusive and most talked about, and strange as it may seem, the mysterious God of Love? Hallelujah, my search was divinely rewarded.

With my prayers for more light and more love, inspirations of first-hand knowledge became my own beyond my wildest dreams. I can confirm with dignity from my heart that what I am about to say to you are not opinions and conclusions of my worldly spirit, but are messages given through me from the spirit of the God of Love. I will write more about my experiences in another chapter. I only want to suggest to you, my readers, that should you find criticism in any subject in my writing to be fair and analyze everything through the spiritual mixing bowl with the cocktail of the virtues of Love. Better yet, take the Word of Jesus, in Matthew 21:22: "And all things, whatsoever ye shall ask in prayer, believing, ye shall receive."

I can also assure anyone out there reading my message that your success will be as good as mine because I am certainly not a man without blemishes. I wish to mention that often, in this religious world of ours, people imagine that you have to be a reverend person to be heard by God. Nothing could be farther from the truth; He will listen to anyone just for the sake of asking. We have been given many a false impression from the pulpit such as not to question God and the Church. I can assure you that God does not mind being questioned and will be pleased that you are sufficiently interested to search for Truth, which is Love.

Jesus said, "Come to me, little children, the Kingdom of Heaven is yours." Jesus so often mentioned, "My Kingdom is not of this world," and when He said, "I am the King of the Jews" He didn't mean to imply that He was a worldly ruler, but a spiritual one. Somehow Christians of today fail to understand that meaning because they are determined that in His next coming He will reign the world's economy and establish peace. I stress to you again that His kingdom is not of this world, but His commandment is the Philosophy of Love. If you fail to live accordingly, He will not know you until you absorb more light and love.

Man has never been closer to His kingdom than you are right now, because by simply asking, you shall receive, was His advice. I have witnessed the cloud of glory, and no worldly experience of a Jesus in a mortal body could possibly match the divine glory of the Christ Spirit. Whenever you are ready for Him, it will fill your heart with overflowing joy and understanding. For those of you who are waiting for His mortality to appear, I say that you are missing out on the greatest experience of your life. Read His Word again and ask for spiritual guidance that you may be enlightened to understand the Truth. There is no greater meeting place anywhere than to meet Him within your own soul, or shall we say, "in the temple of God."

10

Beyond the Mortal Boundaries

In the foregoing chapter, I battled my way between the shores of the body and soul when I tried to familiarize my readers with this divine fact of the universal law, which brings about the duality that we live. It has been generally assumed and taught by some religions that death is the end of both and that science can only prove facts of the conscious five senses of our brain. This is giving us a very close destination or boundary that what Jesus termed "in the flesh" entails all the worldly attributes and accumulations of the mortal body. There is absolutely no doubt in my mind that in death all of the above-mentioned mortality has served its purpose for man and God.

As I previously stated, at the time the Spiritual Soul is released, it will continue to exist according to its brightness in another mansion in the spiritual realm of heaven. The consciousness of the mortal body cannot see beyond the boundaries of nature, but the mind of the Soul has access to vision into eternity. There was a time in my life when the question arose, "Who am I or what am I?" because I, too, saw only one so-called living soul as a human body with con-sciousness fighting for its existence. Eventually, being made aware of continuous reference to the soul of man and the breath of life, there seemed to be a dual relationship between body and soul. I had to find out the truth of this connection because I could not find any satisfactory answers in religion or elsewhere.

I started ringing the bells to receive more light on this important question when, one day, after a month or a few years—I take no note of time—my question was finally answered. The lapse of time seems only like yesterday when, out of the blue, while I was sitting relaxed in my favorite living-room chair, a blanket of white cloud took over my full attention. Slowly the cloud dissolved and a clear panorama unfolded in front of me. I found I was in a country setting and was briskly walking across a yard toward a two-story inn or small hotel.

At both ends of the building, there were open stairs connecting to outside verandas on both floors. Somehow I took the left staircase to the second floor, and upon entering the indoor hallway, I glanced to my right, which was again the connecting hallway to the opposite end of the staircase approximately three room lengths away. Straight ahead, another three rooms away, a stairway was leading down to the lobby. The last room on the left was mine.

As I mentioned, upon entering, while looking to the right, two men were staring toward me from the end of that hallway. Somehow I sensed grave danger because it looked as though they were waiting for me, and I noticed one arm coming up drawing a gun. Scared, I raced forward, and decided against entering my room because a fast glance verified that they were chasing me. I flew down the steps toward the lobby, and at the end of the staircase to the right, I ran into the porter's office. I pulled my wallet out of my pocket and handed it to the porter, asking him to send it to my mother. At about the same instant, the two men were in front of me and fired their pistols point blank and two slugs penetrated my heart. For an instant they looked at me and then disappeared while I was sinking to the floor and falling onto my back.

Immediately, a few people came running and looked down at me, asking the porter what had happened and he told them, "They shot him." I was able to see them, but I could not talk. I felt my hot blood flowing out of my body, and my vision slowly became blurred. I noticed a man pushing his way through the people around me and bending down beside me. He lifted my hand, feeling my pulse, and at this moment I still felt my blood flowing, but by now my vision was slowly disappearing. I could hear someone asking again, "How is he?" And the person holding my hand said, "I think he is dead." I thought to myself dreamily, *How can they say that because I am still conscious, but am unable to move, speak, or see any more?*

All of a sudden, I was looking down from a short distance away to about six people and saw a man holding the hand of a body lying there on the floor. At that moment, the man said again, "He is dead." He dropped the hand he was holding.

Immediately I recognized the body as mine, but there was no more connection of feeling. I was in a state of surprise and confusion, being able to reason and survey the scene of the people milling around, yet my body was lying there apart from me with no attached feelings. Analyzing my predicament, I realized that I still possessed all my faculties, sight, and hearing, but at the same time, I was beginning to sense that the people were unaware of my presence and I was unable to attract their attention. Lo and behold, a bright light appeared, unfolding the knowledge that I was the soul and there lay my assassinated corpse.

I marvelled and looked again toward my lifeless remains with the people surrounding it, and I began to understand that I was the soul ego that used to reside in that body.

Somehow, a content and confident feeling flowed through me and I thought, *Now I know the Truth of the living soul and its duality.*

Again, I surveyed the situation of the body lying there, and the soul separated from it, being me in complete awareness of its existence. Taking it all in, over and over again, I somehow felt deep regrets that I could not share this truth of knowledge, which had now been proven to me, with those left behind. While I was pondering over this great revelation, a white cloud engulfed my presence, then, just as quickly, it began to disperse. Suddenly, right in front of my eyes, the living room began to materialize and—feeling overwhelmed with surprise and somehow shock—I found myself seated in my comfortable chair.

Sitting there, it began to dawn on me that this particular occurrence was a spiritual vision of a previous transition of my soul. For years, I had a yearning in my heart to know the truth regarding the duality of the living soul. After being enriched with this enlightenment, another great principle under the laws of God had been added to my knowledge. A feeling of great joy and peace enclosed my body, lasting for days, and I can truly say that the measure was filled to overflowing.

Now I am here telling you of my experience, and from the depth of my soul, I can confess that the duality of man is no fiction but is a birthright and an inheritance that will express itself in unison as a living soul. This reality cannot change as long as the necessity of rebirth will aid mankind toward the great goal of harmony. The utopia in creation is for the living soul to live the Philosophy of Love under the canopy of the God of Love.

11

God's Spirit within You

"Verily, verily, I say unto you, He that believeth in me, the works that I do shall he do also, and greater works than these shall he do; because I go unto my Father" (John 14:12). I believe the above passage to be one of the greatest statements for us to show that He was the beginning and not the end of the Word, which clearly agrees to man's great spiritual potential "if" we follow His teachings. He stresses repetitiously that this great knowledge is not of Himself but the inspiration from His Father (Holy Spirit). In a humble way, He tells us that we, too, can do the same—search within and find the Truth.

He said, "Follow me, I am the Truth and the Light of this world, I am the Way, because of me your sins shall be forgiven," and note the statement He made, "I and my Father are one." All these proclamations were not meant to make Himself an equal with God but rather to show that He was in complete harmony with the gospel He proclaimed. He truly believed that all His wisdom was from the God of Love, therefore rightly claiming to be in tune with the Father. His greatness was demonstrated to the world through His infallible works: healing the sick and recalling the souls of the dead to the living. All those miracles, He tells us, happened because of faith. Such phenomenal talents have never before, nor since, been demonstrated in all history.

It is quite understandable for mortals to be intimidated

by it and to proclaim Him as God, which the Christians do. Similarities happened to other famous prophets, such as Buddha, Krishna, Muhammad, etc.; as late as World War II, some isolated tribes believed it was the coming of the gods when they saw the airplanes and their vapour trails in the sky. Gods in the past, and even now, are in the eye and comprehension of the beholder.

It is not uncommon in religions and cults, even in Christianity, to practice idolism. Mortal man seems to find comfort in a worldly creation of a god figurine he can see. Creations of many kinds are used for close association, such as altars, crosses, books, paintings and figurines of saints and gods, which seem indispensable to our religions. Religions have learned the ultimate in sensual knowledge: theology begins and ends with the churches' doctrines. An offering of a big cheque is still considered a great spiritual action by them. I am aware that most congregations have great faith in their beliefs and are content and happy. I know, because I was one of them.

Somehow I could never accept that a living soul upon death turns into dust with no spiritual residue whatsoever. This is taught by many Christian churches. They study the Bible with all their senses, but unfortunately, for lack of understanding, they cannot connect man to a spiritual soul. I might add this is the very essence in the teachings of Christ to enlighten man thereof. If you don't believe in a spiritual soul, Jesus had this to say: "Even the spirit of Truth whom the world cannot receive because it seeth Him not, neither knoweth Him: but ye know Him, for He dwelleth with you, and shall be in you."

The Spirit of Truth is our spiritual soul, which can relay to us all knowledge ever experienced by it in the mansions of God. This created individualized unit of God projection is entered into a newborn baby upon its first breath. This creation of duality is then called the living soul. It is the only way the soul can express itself through a mortal body in this physical world. This is why we have so many references stressing the fact of a dual being, for example, "Man does not live on bread alone." I am certain that this statement is giving us unanimous agreement for our need of love, sleep, prayers and song and music to lift, so to speak, our spirit. We do know that the rejuvenation of our will and body through those mediums is as important to the Living Soul as is the daily intake of our food and drink.

"Know ye not that ye are the temple of God, and that the spirit of God dwelleth in you? for the temple of God is holy, which temple ye are" (1 Cor. 3: 16–17). The spiritual presence of our soul is mentioned so often; only the spiritual dead could be ignorant of it. Listen to the next verse: "Love God with all thy heart, and with all thy understanding, and with all thy soul, and with all thy strength" (Mark 12:30).

Did you notice that the three most important and different human attributes were mentioned in the above description? There was no need for Him to refer to the soul as well if it wasn't a separate and important part of man. I understand it to mean that we should love God with body and soul. The Bible tells us that God's Spirit is within. That means that the soul is the conduit for spiritual communication and contains the Book of Life and Truth of all things that will be opened into you. I have asked and have received, and so can you. Apply your spiritual mixing bowl and your salvation is at hand.

The Holy Spirit

The Holy Spirit is the medium between God and the living souls in comfort, in word and in action. Jesus referred to it as

His Father, the Holy Ghost, Spirit, or Truth. When John baptized Jesus, it was said that He received the Holy Ghost. Because of that occurrence, the title of Christ was bestowed upon Him, and so, to this day, some call it the Christ consciousness. We could also call it the glory of God or the fountain of Truth.

The Holy Spirit is not an institution set up for religion,or only for men in "sheep's clothing," but it is the birthright of every living soul.

Look at John 14:7–31. In verse 10, Jesus says, "I speak not of myself; but of the Holy Spirit that dwelleth in me." Verse 12 continues, "Believe in me [teachings], the works I do you can do also." Verses 15 and 16 declare, "If ye love me, keep my commandments." He will send the Comforter to us, and proclaim that even the Spirit of Truth will dwell in us. In Verse 26, He says the Comforter is the Holy Ghost, and in Verse 28 Jesus says, "My Father is greater than I."

Jesus never pretended to be God. He is telling us how He is guided by the Holy Spirit within Him and encourages us to follow those teachings, or the Philosophy of Love, and He says, "The Holy Spirit will be with you also, and forever." It is the path to the glory of knowledge, to peace and happiness for all "Living Souls."

Holy Spirit

O spirit of Love, your light brightens the soul,
 Its radiant heat, flexing the hearts of man.
Bringing forth, to the spiritual mixing bowl,
Affection, and virtues of love, Amen.

Worldly Spirit

A cry, the first breath has taken place,
A miracle, performed by the waves of vibrations.
Filling the lungs, with the fresh air from space,
Activating the heart, the senses, of man creation.
He sees, hears, feels; also can taste and smell,
Those actions stir reactions and register in the brain.
This storehouse is called a memory but how can we tell,
Because its worldly spirit called mind recalls again and
    again.
This wonderful functioning of body and mind,
Proclaims to man this perfect combination, made to meas-
    ure.
Regardless of morality he believes to be the chosen kind,
Without recourse pursuing greed, power and pleasure.
These are the seeds mankind has kept on sowing,
Its harvest was never sweet, but crime, wars, and sorrow.
Darkness instead of light has enclosed the mortal being,
Wake up, without the soul there will be no better tomor-
    row.

In accepting the Philosophy of Love, we are repenting, and whilst practicing this lifestyle, salvation is taking its course. Our soul will again be brightened to give us inspirational guidance, which is rightfully our birthright.

All the spiritual arts pertaining to our senses and mind are, in their nature, of the worldly spirit, such as seances, hypnotism, mind reading, fortune telling of any kind, and all other arts of spiritualism, including all religious traditions. These are activities that can attract good or evil messages; therefore they are of the worldly spirit. It is important for us to understand from whence the message came; this can be established by applying the spiritual mixing bowl. The Holy

Spirit cannot be possessed nor controlled by any being; it will only inspire eternally according to the grace of God. On the other hand, the worldly spirit can successfully be mastered with the harmonious cooperation between body and soul; hence the saying "Nothing is impossible."

12

Visit from Beyond

Late one night during a reposing mood of contemplation, I suddenly became aware of a white cloud surrounding me. This aroused my attention, and I became very observant when the white cloud slowly dispersed in front of my eyes, gradually exposing a scene that quickly became very clear. A beautiful young woman in a long gown who was standing at the top of a stairway started to descend slowly toward me. I immediately became aware of the familiar surroundings as being part of the house I grew up in. The woman started greeting me and enquired of my well-being, and as soon as she spoke, I recognized my mother's voice. At that instant I became very startled and could hardly speak, but I did manage to ask, "How are you, Mother?"

I wish to mention here that my mother had passed away approximately one month before this occurrence. She appeared very radiant and looked as though she was in her late teens instead of a frail, seventy-seven-year-old lady. I was totally mystified when she said, "I came to tell you that everything is fine with me and things are wonderful where I am." She was smiling and then said, "Your belief is the Truth, follow it always." Those remarks astonished me to no end because during her lifetime, we never discussed my beliefs and hadn't met for the past twelve years. Her encouragement gave me immense happiness and instilled great confidence in me to continue in the "Philosophy of Love." She also told me that she would contact as many people as possible to let them know that she is happy. We had a few more exchanges; then I popped another question, which I believe caused our parting. She did not answer me, and at that instant, the white cloud closed in again and she disappeared.

The living room scene unfolded once more in front of my eyes where I remained for hours contemplating this wonderful and exciting vision that I had just experienced. No words can fully describe or do justice to such a phenomenon. The associated joyful feeling remained with me for several days afterwards. I had a great feeling that another principle was proven to me, which mystery has perplexed mankind throughout the ages. If there is any doubt in your mind about the continuation of our spiritual soul or afterlife (whatever terminology you want to use), I can assure you that there is a celestial realm, the true home of our soul. This spiritual abode is giving us the only satisfactory conclusion because the rhythm of the cosmos and the continuation of the soul in another mansion is under the grace of the Holy Spirit.

"In my Father's house there are many mansions," was the proclamation of Jesus, and we should be aware by now that His Father, to whom he referred so often, is the Holy Spirit. The mansion of the soul from whence my mother came was the realm where the brightness of the soul reflects into the appearance of the entity. I can attest that her life was all goodness, and I do not believe that any of my brothers and sisters could say anything different. My mother had a hard life, a heart of gold, and nothing but kindness to give. Her appearance gave me the answer to spiritual justice here on earth and thereafter, and many more principal and cosmic laws were opened unto me. I often wish that such an experience would happen to me again, but I realize her important mission to enlighten me has been fulfilled.

I only hope that my translation of holy principles and

laws is doing justice to their importance. We are being continually bombarded by the worldly spirit of greed and lust, but understanding life will give us the strength and will to overcome the distraction of evil. The spiritual mixing bowl will help us do the right things if we value a higher standard of morality and a better life in general. We cannot give a greater inheritance to future generations than the morality standard created by living in the Philosophy of Love.

Spiritual Love

Spiritual love is in living and by upholding all the virtues there are: respect, justice, goodness, righteousness, integrity, conscientiousness, uprightness, etc. By keeping all the virtues in the course of action in our life, a person truly represents the Philosophy of Love, and it is by this acceptance that we establish the morality standard of a people. The spiritual love does not require the emotions of our sentiment; instead it needs only the commitment of truth from within. A continuous performance of upholding truth is the highest accomplishment for the living soul to achieve.

The laws of love are of the Holy Spirit and its seeds and harvest will be fulfilled to bring peace and harmony to all those who practice the Philosophy of Love. Spiritual love can be regulated or enforced by making it the country's constitution, and by its practice, it will derive a high morality standard in such a land. The spiritual mixing bowl is our blessing whereby we establish our present and future behavior in life. It will also reestablish the principle of balance between body and soul when our destiny will once again be in the light of the living as intended in the Book of Life.

Spiritual Love

Spiritual Love comes from within, it yearns for justice and
  respect,
It teaches us to uphold the Truth and the evils to reject.
The laws of Love are stirring and enlightening our soul,
Giving us awareness to make the right choices through the
  mixing bowl.
This will bring happiness and joy for all living things,
If we do not have it we must pray for its blessings.
Righteousness and morality of which the world has not
  enough,
That is why we are urged the lifestyle in the Philosophy of
  Love.

Family Love

I think it is important for people to differentiate between and
to understand the various aspects of love. Most of us were
raised in the environment of a loving family circle in which
spiritual love is taken for granted and sentimental emotions
are interwoven in various degrees. Our feelings are often
distorting reality, and hypocritical judgements can override
and interfere with such love. Emotions aren't stable and often
interfere with spiritual love because the overwhelming influence of the worldly spirit is greed and power. To stabilize
family love, we must make use of the spiritual mixing bowl,
which makes us aware of the destructive evil influences in
our lives. If we sacrifice spiritual love for whatever reason,
we are guilty of causing inner frustration in ourselves and
other living souls, which will then reflect into a lower morality standard of a society. Family love can be extended without trust, whereas spiritual love is built on trust.

Family Love

The mother, father, sister or brother are our family and so
    close,
We love, adore and help them and always abide by our
    vows.
If this were true we would have reached utopia and love
    would treat us kind,
But here on earth are realities which depend on our frame
    of mind.
We struggle for more power and thereby enhance greed,
Our worldly demand is always more than we need.
Because of those wants family love so often has lost its
    affection,
We must pray for spiritual love and meet excesses with
    rejection.
The spiritual mixing bowl will balance those troubles
    above,
And keep us on the path in the Philosophy of Love.

Sensual Love

All living creatures in this world, including mankind, by
coming of age will experience a sexual awakening from
within. In the animal kingdom, this is usually, as we know
it, experienced at a certain period of the year. This necessary
principle and law of nature is responsible for the continual
reproduction of all species of our planet. Those occurrences
by mankind are termed love, and the result of courtship is
marriage in today's human society. Because of its involving
pleasures, it has become a year-round recreation between
both sexes. The hormones responsible create the most intense
power in our human system and all our senses seem to be
affected toward that direction.

However, as misdirected as our senses might be, this

100

vitality is applicable for use in everything we undertake in our lives. People have been brainwashed for eons of time that a happy marriage depends upon a continuous sex life in order to have a lasting relationship. Here is where love has found its greatest distortion because sex is considered to be love, and for so many people, that is their conclusion. Young teenagers are manipulated into sex because they are told, "If you love me, then prove it." This confusion in not knowing the difference between sex and love has created more heartbreak and problems in this world than any other cause. More than half of the marriages today are failing because of mistaken love and this artificial foundation is crumbling with the waning of sexual desire. This frequent activity and the emotions involved are strictly sensual and of the worldly spirit.

Therefore, if we like to see marriage as a godly union between man and wife, spiritual love and family love must also be present. Without the two, sensual love of attraction will not survive to see happiness in a joint union. The courtship ritual for a potential marriage must be analyzed through the spiritual mixing bowl. In doing so, we will find the Truth from within and this assurance will give us confidence, happiness, and a trusting relationship with our chosen partner.

Sensual Love

There was no soul when the eyes fell in love at first sight,
They have chosen a partner to make love the very next
    night.
They caressed and kissed and professed love indeed,
The soul was never consulted but only the sexual need.
The pleasure was great but the romance was short,
The desire started to dwindle and then they became bored.
 So love started to crumble in its dire plight,

It had no foundation and no guiding light.

Married Love

Adam and Eve looked after Eden and together they cared,
Beholding a tree they plucked an apple which they shared.
Married life has ups and downs and there are rules to heed,
They must help together and have concerns of each other's
    need,
This partnership is for life and calls for oneness with no ex-
    ception,
Sensual love is now important and to share affection.
But to the soul family love and spiritual love must now be
    the foundation.
Because the Philosophy of Love is the only lifestyle worthy
    of recognition.

13

Rebirth

Some people call it reincarnation, a subject that seems to be extremely controversial. There are many religions around the world that hold rebirth of the soul as a natural doctrine. Many references of this phenomena are made in the Old Testament, and Jesus Himself referred to it quite frequently.

First, we must understand and accept the fact that we exist as a body and soul. The spiritual ego of man is attracted and incorporated into the physical body upon the newborn baby's first breath, hence the term "the Breath of Life." This established duality of the spirit and the flesh was then called "the living soul." Because the soul itself is invisible and our senses cannot perceive it, it is, therefore, considered not existing. In combination with the body, it can express itself and perform a mission it contemplated, or was granted, by the grace of God. This combined duality has mystified mankind ever since, because the real purpose of existence was not only for the mortal body but for the soul to experience.

This awareness has been clouded by the predominant nature of our sensual mind, which is the underlying cause of the worldly spirit. Education is very important to this living soul, but, unfortunately, in the process, the worldly mind was not satisfied alone by feeding and clothing the body. There were temptations for excesses, so greed and lust became the goal for success. Our soul became obscured and was not consulted further because its morality was not in harmony with evil tidings. Occasionally an inspired being would try to influence his followers with love in order to retune their wayward lifestyles.

We can see from our past history how love was treated shabbily and merely used as a convenient tool to gain more power and for self-glorification. People's words spoke of love, but their actions were from the Devil himself. Out of these flickers of light and hellish darkness, organizations were born that we today call religions. As of now, they are unable to confine the spiritual threshold between the worldly spirit that carries good and evil, versus the Holy Spirit that only carries love. This unfortunate confusion has created a world of low morality whose fruits are wars, pestilence, and disease. It is my hope that my inspirations will enlighten others and resurrect their soul back into the driver's seat to bring change with the Philosophy of Love.

Our soul is committed until the death of our body to initiate salvation with the actions of love, thereby erasing the evil engravings in our soul. So often the question stirring in our heart is, "What is the purpose of our existence?" This mystery has been termed by religion as being "unexplainable and only God knows the cause and purpose" of our being here.

I agree that it has not been fully explained because man has never sounded the bells to the God of Love to enquire into its mystery. I have tirelessly knocked on the Door in the fashion that Jesus encouraged us to do, and His Word did not fail. Our soul in the image of the light is a miniscule co-creator of this abstract, sensual world. Its influence is a holy venture if it is not tainted and darkened by the worldly spirit of wickedness. Everyone in this world has his role to accomplish in order to brighten our soul and to be accountable again in our next stage of our continuous cycle.

Early theologians and philosophers maintained that the

souls of man are continually created as needed, but this I know was not inquired of the Holy Spirit. It was only an assumption by the short sight of not understanding the existence of the soul. I dispute their statement in proclaiming bluntly that we are recycled souls and all were created before the world began. The creation of the universe is an abstract of the spiritual realm of the souls, and therefore only the physical appearances and bodies were created when the Scriptures describe the creation of the world.

In Titus 1:2 it states: "In hope of eternal life, which God, that cannot lie, promised before the world began"; so if there were no souls, to whom did God make that promise? Bodies, after all, did not exist before the beginning of this sensual world.

In the Book of Job, we find another interesting description referring to the pre-world era. In Job 38:4–7 we read: "When the morning stars sang together, and all the sons of God shouted for joy." In the realm of the souls, there was no evil, therefore they are all referred to as the sons of God in this caption.

There is a continuation of this spiritual world apart from our worldly abstract when Jesus proclaimed in John 14:2, "In my Father's house are many mansions: if it were not so, I would have told you. I go and prepare a place for you." He is not talking of an earthly place but of a heavenly one, nor is He talking of this earth when He said in verse 3, "And if I go and prepare a place for you, I will come again, and receive you unto myself; that where I am, there ye may be also." This is not an earthly dialogue of His physical Second Coming as so widely believed, but is strictly a spiritual destination for our soul.

Rebirth has been widely disputed and so often denied by the Christian clergy; they bluntly deny that such a divine law exists. In fact, this law is the greatest principle of justice in the Book of Life. Without this advent there would be no purpose for salvation and a Redeemer would be useless if the time for correction is not at hand or in a future cycle of life. So many are cut short, others don't make it past a baby stage or childhood, and those who cause terror for others will meet the laws of karma. Jesus warned that they will pay to the last farthing.

The nature of sin is of the sensual world because it cannot transcend and be used in the mansions of the soul and therefore must be redeemed and compensated where they originated. This is the eternal law of justice, which will not change for the sake of man, neither will elaborate traditions have any effect to change this course. The only healing power will be our prayers for more light and more love, thereby gaining the wisdom to start compensation now and to live in the Philosophy of Love.

The human faculty of comprehending life makes it difficult to see justice in the unfair distribution of equality. One is born rich and the other poor; one healthy and the other sick; one will experience a long life and another a short one. If there is but one life cycle, then I admit fairness would not, and could not, be served. Everlasting hell fire for the wicked and eternal glory for the good are both lacking spiritual justice and purpose. Those visions are incredulous and barbaric and do not fulfill a niche in creation, or otherwise. Life on earth will always be a cycle, which does not extend into eternity, but greater goals of cocreating will be in store for those who overcome the worldly spirit and relish in self-mastery and faith.

Jesus represents to Christians, and anyone else who wants to listen, an exemplary image of God's will in action. He enlightened us of love and proved to us with His word, in life and in His death, valuable principles of eternal laws. I am satisfied in the knowledge that reincarnation is in the law

106

of Creation and does not yield to worldly ambitions. This gives the soul ego another chance to prepare, and if need be, have another beginning preconceived for the glory or damnation to overcome and master once more the cycle of a living soul on this earth. There will be great mysteries ahead for the soul in transit because we do not know which one of the many mansions will be our resting place.

In the doctrine of Jesus, many commentaries were made by Him in reference to the content of the spiritual soul; therefore, I shall no longer enlarge upon its existence. Instead, I will focus on some fascinating statements made by the Master Jesus regarding reborn souls. He demonstrated His knowledge of this most important principle of life, and so did His apostles. There was an episode in John 9:1–4 in which the apostles passed a man on the street whom everybody knew was born blind. They asked Jesus, "Master, who did sin, this man, or his parents, that he was born blind?" Jesus answered, "Neither has this man sinned nor his parents: but that the works of God should manifest in him."

The important thing here is how the question was asked! The disciples distinctly stated that the man was born blind. How could this man have possibly sinned before he was born, unless they all believed that he could have sinned in a previous life and karma was the result of his predicament? Of course, there is the second possibility that his parents had sinned and he became blind by inheritance due to venereal disease or drug abuse. Neither of the foregoing factors were responsible when Jesus said, "But that the works of God should manifest in him."

This demonstrates the third possibility for a birth defect that could have resulted from a preconceived plan of the soul's intentions and time of its impending journey. It must be noted that Jesus did not rebuke their question, but I am certain He would have done if rebirth would not have been in the Book of Life. It was compatible with His teachings, so He promptly stated that neither had sinned. I assure you that Jesus would never have missed the opportunity of correcting His disciples if they had expressed in any way an important principle in the wrong fashion.

Matthew 16:13 states: "When Jesus came into the coasts of Caesarea Philippi, He asked His disciples, saying, Whom do men say that I the Son of Man am?" In verse 14 they say, "Some say that thou art John the Baptist: some, Elias; and others, Jeremias, or one of the prophets." The above is directly referring to rebirth because the populace in those days expected a great prophet to be a reborn son of divine lineage, and they wanted to know of what reincarnation He was. This discussion would not have taken place if there was no such thing as rebirth.

Luke 9:7–9 explains: "Now Herod the tetrarch heard of all that was done by him: and he was perplexed, because that it was said of some, . . . that Elias had appeared; and of others, that one of the old prophets was risen again. And Herod said, John have I beheaded: but who is this of whom I hear such things? And he desired to see him." If a man like Herod knew about and believed in rebirth, then there is absolutely no doubt that the knowledge of reincarnation was no mystery, but an accepted occurrence.

Note Matthew 17:10–13. To keep this description brief, I will only mention part of verses 12 and 13: "But I say unto you, that Elias is come already, and they knew him not, but have done unto him whatsoever they listed. Then the disciples understood that He spake unto them of John the Baptist."

Once before, Jesus had referred to this episode in Matthew 11:12–15. Verse 14 states: "And if ye receive it, this is Elias, which was for to come." He was uncertain whether or not His disciples understood that Elias was the rebirth of

John the Baptist, but in Matthew 17:13, they indicated that they understood immediately that he was referring to John. Rebirth is a principle under the law of creation, and life as a duality of body and soul does make sense. In lieu of this law of karma, it is imperative that we heed its consequences. Then life in the Philosophy of Love becomes worthwhile.

Life on this earth appears to be nothing more than a gamble in our undertakings. Morality seems to be upheld only by the naive because criminality has taken away that lifestyle, and survival is only for the fittest amongst a pack of thieves. As a matter of fact, for humankind I am inclined to maintain that the world has been transformed into a living hell. The Old Testament is full of murderous prophets whom we are supposed to honor, and the pharaohs and kings are still the Lucifers of evil.

If we scan the world the picture is not pleasant; not much has changed and the fires of hell are still consuming innocent people. We have a United Nations with power to curb aggressors immediately if we so desire. They can apply total embargo, and if this does not work within one month, then the option must be to destroy their war machinery totally, and in earnest. Yugoslavia and many other places are hell in action. We are boasting to be peacekeepers, and yet we allow them to kill innocent women and children in front of our mighty forces. If love and respect of life is not worthwhile to interfere with, then there is no reason to have a United Nations force.

A small organization like Greenpeace, for example, was able to stop seal hunting and other undertakings the world over. I would think that approximately two billion followers of religion throughout the world would be able to stop the human slaughter in so many countries. Is it possible that so many could only be pretenders of the Will of God, which is love? They are sitting by and letting it happen as though no one cares.

Religious beliefs are due to rejuvenate and put centuries of derailment back on track. Love is the power and wisdom that has the strength and courage to accomplish that. Mixed with honesty and justice, the world can rebound from the present horrors to the lifestyle in the Philosophy of Love. This is the plan written in heaven for those we term the human race. There is no other commandment emanating from the Holy Spirit than to follow the eternal Will, which is Love.

"Go and multiply" is the command and process under the laws of nature. The principal of copulation is the sole responsibility according to the species. Man has a great advantage in this co-creation because of his intellect, foresight, and possible awareness of the soul. This spiritual entity enters the earthly body at birth upon the first breath. This miracle passes as a worldly phenomenon, but in actuality from here on, we are a duality of the body and the soul.

Jesus referred to this as the flesh and the spirit but mentioned frequently the importance of the soul. The laws affecting the co-creation of life are perfect and will never change. To fulfill those laws as intended, they depend entirely on the morality standard of the people involved. We have progressed sufficiently in our society to realize the importance of health and married love in order to have and raise children successfully. If there is any deviation from the heterosexual act or excesses, the consequences are never far behind. Children also suffer if there is marriage failure, drunkenness, drugs, adultery, and sexual deviations.

It has been said and proven in medicine, that the sins of the forefathers can be inherited or transmitted into the third and fourth generation. Take into consideration that this has been going on for millenniums. Therefore is it any wonder that we have people who claim to be born with various unnatural sexual orientations? Just because we have a large number of people afflicted by the sins of the forefathers does not mean that it is God-given, as so widely accepted.

A society may approve of those deviations because of pressure and false beliefs, but the eternal laws will never adjust, or accept, such behaviour. Human beings are solely responsible for the health of our offsprings, and we should not place the burden or blame on God. He made the laws for us to uphold, and if we obey, we will be blessed to live in the Philosophy of Love.

14

Sins to Reckon

The accumulation of sins may be so horrendous that in one lifetime we do not have sufficient time to compensate for them. Our soul will definitely carry the imprint with it into another reincarnation, but in the meantime, the brightness of our soul will have dimmed accordingly. This state of darkness is unfortunate upon transition because in the spiritual realm the light of love is equal to the five senses in our worldly domain. There will be a time for these self-inflicted sufferings to take place and for justified reckonings to occur.

The law of karma was established by God with intense love and foresight to purify and compensate for errors committed. For example, your body has a liver to neutralize impurities taken in by the eating and drinking process. We know there are limitations on this organ; delivered poisoning and excessive drug and alcohol abuse will therefore cause sickness, or even death. This exemplifies the folly of man. All kinds of self-made sufferings befall the human race continuously, including wars, famine, and global pollution.

To rectify all the above worldly problems, we must have the input of all the countries of the world in order to heed the law, "All for one and one for all." Our green forests throughout the world have a similar function as the example of the liver process above. The air carries and settles the impurities thereon, whipped by wind and washed into the soil by the rain, and new springs come forth with the life-sustaining clean water. The last hundred years of industrial revolution have proven to us the disregard of man's harmonious existence with nature. We have ravaged the forests and failed to replace the seedlings, and poisonous chemicals are spilled into the air and the fresh water streams around this globe.

Take heed, the race for power and greed has just begun, but man has already grossly overstepped his bounds and abused the fertility of the land and therefore must find a recourse. Sewage and spills are already clogging the arteries of all great rivers in this world. Wildlife and fish are choking to death with slime, which makes us wonder about the spread of other diseases. We are constantly praying to God for better health and wealth and yet, at the same time, we continue to destroy His rose garden of creation upon which our life and health depend. The great religions of the world have failed to raise a finger to stop the greatest sin of all time, "pollution."

Because of this reckless neglect in the world, I am pressed in my soul to heed the call in this age of challenge to add one more addition to our ten commandments: "Ye shall not pollute and destroy God's creation." All other commandments are violated if this new one is not fulfilled.

Sins are the weaknesses in the will of man, driven by the selfish motives of lust and greed. Those strong forces then become the main goal for our senses to achieve. We must strongly desire to overcome the excesses of the flesh in order to lead a life of human respect and decency. Greed and lust have ravaged man of his virtues, and he is forever more plunging himself deeper and deeper into spiritual poverty. Many children and adults of all ages are possessed by the ever present demon of drugs, making their lives a shambles and meaningless. Why has such senseless self-destruction interfered with the lives of so many? Where are the answers?

Is it fair to point a finger toward the educational system, or lack of it? Is our emphasis on greed our downfall?

What about the religions of the world? Have they failed to bring rejuvenation and truth to strengthen the hearts of the followers? Religions are very much concerned with the strict adherence to their selected teachings and rituals of old, but nothing is open to question; only acceptance is the law. Today we have a choice: take it or leave it. But even that choice was not always open. Holy wars and killing of opponents with different faiths is recorded throughout history, and even in this day, we have countries where such inhuman acts are considered a divine law.

In general, most people belonging to one church or another have been raised in that faith since childhood. Their parents' and grandparents' attendance might be traced back for a thousand years or more, having never learned anything different. Because of this inborn dependency and social obligation, it was easy for religion to keep those people in line. Many of those habitual followers cannot recall what is preached from the pulpit because, for them, the importance of church lies in their attendance only. Somehow they feel security in the great social multitude.

I have nothing against churches; they are great social organizations who keep their congregations together with a kindred spirit. They are the richest organizations throughout the world, "even after tax," because they do not have to pay any! Their businesses extend and compete with tax-paying corporations, from banks to farms, from resource industries to real estate—you name it, they have it! Television, of course, has not only made Hollywood famous, it equally famed the TV evangelists.

Have you ever listened to the messages they bring across? Of course you listened, and it all sank in, because the first thing you did after the show was write them a cheque to fulfill their "message." Their gift of the gab has made old women cry, and it is a cinch for them to put Jesus on the auction block. There is never enough to give to Jesus because He loves you, and He gives you tenfold in return. How about this one: "We hope that our prayers today will take care of our accumulated bills—God bless you for your generosity."

Another great evangelist was selling anointing oil, packaged from salad oil, to 300,000 Canadian senior citizens. The packages contained a fitting message, asking the recipients to bless their money with it and to send him the biggest cheque or dollar bill they have. Anyone complying, he promised, would be blessed with financial security.

Another dandy from the gift of the gab. This evangelist asked his donors to give to the "bank of God" where he promised a hundredfold return. For an investment of $100, God would return $10,000. This one beats them all: "I am praying and fasting in my ivory tower because my life is threatened by the assassin God. He gave me orders to raise seven million dollars for my pet project and if I fail—dear me—help, help, help!" The wimp is still alive, and, you guessed it, he got the money. After all, his project is important! It will educate high-income people in his university with a sure clone return of at least ten percent for ever and ever. There is a rosy future for the upper echelon of mammon.

What would Jesus say to all this? You blasphemous hypocrites, God didn't get a penny from your collections, and as long as children are dying of hunger around the world, you have given Him nothing. So many gifted speakers of the pulpit preach the gospel mainly for monetary gain rather than teaching the Philosophy of Love. Is there a genuine reason to collect money in the name of God or Jesus Christ in a time of world hunger and distress? I do not believe there is a genuine reason to collect money in the name of God or

Jesus unless the collections are all donated to alleviate the suffering peoples of this world.

Listen, all of you out there: those preaching the slogan, "Accept Jesus today and all your sins are forgiven," are actually not listening to His teachings but misrepresenting the true message. Like the bird in the cage that promises all his fellow inmates that all their sins are forgiven, they are just not spreading the teachings of Jesus.

This misunderstanding is derived from the crucifixion because it signifies that He died for the sins of man. This statement is quite true, but the ring of it has a different meaning. Jesus knew and believed the true word of God, and He also knew that those who follow His message would truly be purified and would therefore sin no more. If you follow the script and live by it, He can rightly claim that He died for your sins. Not until you follow in His doctrine are those sins in the making erased. He always said, "Go and sin no more."

Now that still leaves us with the old sins of the past. How long do you have to sin no more in order to compensate for them? One good deed may erase a misdemeanor, but there are also unshakeable established laws to compensate for such evils—I should call them karma—and allow me to remind you that we will pay to the last farthing.

The great fortunes that are amassed by the holy pretenders include the power they seek and the power they exercise over the young, the meek, and the blind followers. Many of their messages are mottled, entwined with evil and love, and confuse the souls, even of the very elect. They hold their renowned status amongst men as proof that their riches are the blessings bestowed upon them by God. Jesus acknowledged their splendour on the outside but proclaimed that inside they are like raving wolves. They walked pitilessly over the unfortunate carcasses of children who died of hunger. Never has more arrogance been demonstrated. Take

116

heed of this message of Christ: "No one shall come in but by me, or those who do the Will of my Father which is in Heaven."

Morality is the valor in life, the number-one virtue man must learn and adhere to. References to morality should be taught in schools. Parents always hope their children will grow up with strong moral characters because society builds its hope and future upon this. In every segment of society, man is judged by it, regardless of educational background. The doctrine deserves and needs much more attention by mankind.

Newspaper headlines are full of shattered moral principles, and those perverting them come from all walks of life. It is distressing to see people in trust, such as politicians, who are voted and chosen by the people, and then discover their inefficiencies and self-serving traits. Nobody likes to hire a man or woman of low character (whatever that means) for any kind of business, nor does a person appreciate such a so-called friend. It is clearly established that skills cannot override trust.

It has been said by Jesus that it will be hard for a rich man to enter heaven, because of his all-glorified power and greed. We are aware that few have reached great wealth with compassion and love. No matter how far back we research in history, morality is a word similar to God, the leaders and kings having molded and enforced it to their liking. Morality is the key to human rights, but shamefully it is still abused in many countries and the victims are young children. Slavery is a good example: this has been outlawed in the Western cultures for some time but still festers in the underworld. For thousands of years, it was a product for trade and it is still practised in some countries around the globe.

How can governments and religions of today allow this to continue, and show no feelings for such transactions in open marketplaces? It boggles our minds to think of such a horrible existence for the unfortunate children involved. They were, and are still, bought by the rich and affluent in society to be used on plantations, and in factories and brothels all over the world. Everybody was, and is, aware of this, especially today with all the media coverage. Even the prophets and the lords of ancient times were aware of this, and, of course, no religion was ignorant of it, nor are they today.

Authorities demanded that slaves be treated well, but ironically no one insisted on abolishing such human degradation. Why? They professed love in those days too, just as they do today, and it still remains only a word to preach and not to uphold. The above-described slavery of children still exists in many countries and will continue to exist as long as world governments and religions condone it. They, alone, have the influence and power to teach the Philosophy of Love; only when this is taught will world miseries start to decline accordingly on this planet. The abuse of spiritual love is ignored the world over and is directly connected with the low morality everywhere. We must use the spiritual mixing bowl and allow love to lead our way because love alone will be the Redeemer and Saviour of this world.

15

The Horrid Gods of Old

Being born into the religious jungle of man, I have stomped through its wilderness for forty years. My eyes and ears were anxious to see or hear of a flicker of light that might herald the success of my journey. The God of Love was my goal, but the light of Truth was nowhere to be found. In desperation, I closed my eyes to shut out the glorification by man.

In this retreat, for the first time in my search, the stirrings of my soul let me know that I was heard. My solitary communion with my soul left me with questions answered and showed me the way to the God of Love through the Holy Spirit. I was fortunate with this occurrence that the resurrection of my soul took place. This innate blessing has opened in me the Book of Life and has allotted the knowledge of many laws and principles pertaining to the living soul. It makes me feel especially worthy that I am chosen to bring and repeat to those who are willing to listen that "Love" is the wisdom of life. There is another important message for this world, that the Philosophy of Love should be the constitution for all humanity.

With these inspired feelings and knowledge, I have since experienced years of a happy balance between my body and soul. The complexity of human life has endless questions, but it is in the pleasure of God to enlighten us thereof and to have the Holy Spirit brighten our soul with inspirational guidance. I am told that the Holy Spirit is the birthright for every living soul in this mansion of the God of Love and possesses the full rights to its wisdom, if so desired. Jesus made it clear to us that in Love all things are fulfilled. If this expectation is true, then it seems reasonable for all Christians to understand that Love is, and must be, a way of life. "Evil," heaven forbid, has never been, and never will be, a trend of the true God as so widely preached and mistakenly accepted in many Christian doctrines. The gods of the times, as I call them, were manlike warriors wantonly killing women and children and causing war and pestilence—those actions are totally void of Love.

For many of us who believe in Love and morality, we rightfully expect common decency amongst all those who preach the ten commandments and represent the many religions around this Western and civilized world. Can we not rely on theology and the deans of high religious places to finally come clean about the evils of the gods they portray? They must tell us why they believe it is all right for God to be unrighteous, jealous, and murderous, causing afflictions and mayhem among the helpless of this world. How do they justify their silence and failure to protest against those atrocities committed by their lords of the past, which is the foundation of their dogmatic beliefs?

The new paraphrased version of the Bible, called the *Living Bible,* is an explicit example of how distortion by changing words can take place. It is full of ridiculous misinterpretations. In Romans 9:9–22 it states: "God has the right to do with His creations as He pleases," as it were, "To hate or love, to bless or curse, to save or kill." In short, He can play darts and we are the target. These games seem endless. Verse 14 says: "Is God being unfair?" "Of course not," is the book's answer; "God has a right to do as He pleases." In verse 20, the queries continue: "Who are you to criticize God?" Should the "creation" say to the "Creator," "Why have you made me like this?" Then in verse 21 there is speculation: when a man makes a jar out of clay doesn't he have the right to use the same lump of clay to make one jar beautiful to be used for holding flowers and another one plain to throw garbage into? Is it not disgusting even to contemplate that all the above lust and power against the people by their man-made gods would be considered normal and righteous? It is highly disturbing that our religious leaders are not even considering the free will given to man whereby they could determine and find the Truth between the rivalry of the gods of evil and the creator of the God of Love.

In the King James version, Exodus 6:3, the Lord said to Moses: "I appeared unto Abraham, unto Isaac, and unto Jacob by the name of God Almighty, but by my name Jehovah was I not known to them." Why, then, does the paraphrased Bible refer to a Jehovah in Genesis 6:3? The Jehovah of Moses may have represented a new beginning and he made himself a deity, continuing in similar ways. Their assumption that this Jehovah was the same Almighty God who appeared to Abraham is distorting the presentation. In those days any ruthless magi and dictator could have achieved such glory with followers like Moses. He did not have love or respect of others but only fulfilled the commands he claimed were from his God.

Another distortion can be found in Genesis 6:1–4. In verse 2 it states: ". . . that the sons of God saw the daughters of man that they were fair; and they took them wives of all which they chose." In verse 1, the *Living Bible* emphasizes a "population explosion," which I believe exaggerates the word of multiplying. This was only meant as an increase of the population. In verse 4 they say that in those days, and even afterwards, the "evil beings from the Spirit World" were sexually involved with human women. This assumption that the Sons of God were evil beings from the spirit world certainly requires some explanation. The spiritual realm that I know of has no evil spirits who can come at will to have sex with earthly women. The only other spirit world which comes to my mind would be the worldly spirit environment of alcohol, which certainly needs clarification.

I didn't realize that the Sons of God were evil beings! Would it be in order to compare father like son? It is amazing that this God had no control over his evil Sons. Since it is assumed that Jehovah was the God from the very beginning, then it would be correct that the Sons of God at that time were his offspring.

In the New Testament, the Sons of God depict a completely different version in Romans 8:14, in which Paul comments, "For as many as are led by the Spirit of God, they are the Sons of God." If the wording of Paul is correct, then it would be a safe assumption that those evil Sons of God were led by an equally evil Jehovah. I am slowly becoming confused, so let us all start thinking for ourselves, so that everyone can figure out this Godly charade.

Here I have another message from my soul; listen to it carefully: "Love must be in harmony with all its virtues, in word and in action, and no other decree has ever been carried by the Holy Spirit. Love is the measuring stick for Truth. Without Love there is no Truth, and where Truth is not present there is no Love." This method of assessment will determine in our hearts if the actions of the gods of man were of the worldly sensual spirit or of the Holy Spirit from the God of Love. It would be naive in this age to be afraid of judging the creed we follow, with the world full of deception around us. Take the advice of Jesus who warned us to be aware of the men in sheep's clothing—they pretend holiness but inside are like raving wolves. Therefore, be not afraid of questioning God for Truth; only charlatans and false prophets will deny you that privilege of questioning their ways and opinions.

All of the above that is outlined makes up a very important description which will ready you for the journey of morality on which I am about to take you. If we read any kind of literature in philosophy, religion, or the Holy Bible etc., we must assess its spiritual content and feel free to analyse and compare to the realities of men in relation to God. We are told that our existence lies in His mercy; therefore, I find it must be of the utmost importance for us to find out if we really are a mere product of fate, and pawns to be kicked around for fun. Gods have been immortalized for thousands of years. Even the sun, the moon, the stars, and all the elements have, at one time or another, served as the gods for mankind; and men, animals, and birds were not left out in the glorifying of a deity. Burnt offerings of flesh and blood provided the pleasing aroma and sacrifice that those gods demanded. Those gods of the times were freely bartering in gold, silver, animals and human lives to satisfy their contempt for humanity. Love, as yet, did not come from those gods but was a word used only in the abyss of deception.

I will cut short the journey we are about to take and will contain it only to a few recent gods of the times mentioned in the Old Testament since the era of Adam and Eve. Genesis 3:1–6 says that God put the Tree of Knowledge into the middle of the Garden of Eden and commanded Adam and Eve not to eat thereof. In conversation with the serpent, the woman decided to eat of the fruit and gave some to her husband and both ate of it. Verse 7 continues:

And the eyes of them were both opened, and they knew that they were naked; (8) And they heard the footsteps of the Lord God walking in the Garden. Adam and Eve hid themselves from the presence of God amongst the trees. (9) And God

123

called Adam, "Where are you?" (10) And he said "I heard thy voice and I was afraid, because I was naked: and I hid myself." (11) "Who told thee that thou wast naked? Hast thou eaten of the tree whereof I commanded thee that thou shouldest not eat?" And Adam blamed Eve for their predicament.

Verses 16–17 continue: "God cursed the woman to greatly multiply the sorrows of childbirth. To Adam, God cursed the ground for much sorrow to find food unto all the days of his life." Because of their sin, the death penalty was extended to all living souls, and so was the sorrowful childbearing and hardship of life established for all time to come.

This story has mystified mankind since its origin, and no one dares to question its purpose and truth. Is it because it appears to be an exaggerated punishment for only one sin committed by two people that all of mankind is punished for ever more? Before resigning myself to the above vengeance of the Lord, I have a few more events to add. This story is in great conflict with Creation because the breath of life was given to mankind through His nostrils upon birth. It has been said that with it was bestowed the free will to man, and—I may add—this tool has the purpose of dividing good from evil. By this action the Tree of Knowledge had already been taken care of; therefore, planting this tree in the middle of the garden was useless and an act of blatant temptation by the Lord (a command without purpose). Such actions are said to be sinful.

It has been said that man was created in the image of God and was given dominion over all things. He also commanded man to multiply, and man was blessed by God. If that is true, then nakedness was no mystery to them nor was it a sin.

Another question arises: why do animals die? They did not eat of the Tree of Knowledge. If it was important for religion to establish the origin of sin, then the Garden of Eden story has surely created a new one. It has brought upon women inequality, slavery, disrespect, and degradation ever since.

The latest renewal of such discrimination was echoed by Saint Paul in Timothy 2:8–15: "Let the woman learn in silence with all subjection, but I suffer not the woman to teach, nor to usurp authority over the man, but to be in silence." This religious stigma against the female gender discourages equality in the eyes of religion until this day. Now you have met the first god of the times on our journey. He cursed mankind with sorrow and death. It will now be up to you to decide in your heart if the actions of the Lord in Eden were made of Love.

We will go next to Genesis 6:2, 4, 9, 13: "That the sons of God saw the daughters of men that they were fair; and they took them wives of all which they chose." Verse 4 states: "When the sons of God came in unto the daughters of men, and they bare children to them, the same became mighty men which were of old, men of renown." If those people were so good, where were they during the Flood? I only recalled the above few verses to throw light on the sons of the gods. Were they the offspring of the gods who walked in the Garden of Eden?

In verse 13, God decided that the world was corrupt and that He would put an end to it all by flooding the world. In verse 9, Noah walked with God, who instructed him how to build the ark, and He ordered Noah to bring his family and one pair of every beast into the ark, and Noah obeyed the orders of God. Genesis 7:11 states: "In the six hundredth year of Noah's life, in the second month, the seventeenth day of the month, the same day were all the fountains of the great deep broken up, and the windows of heaven were opened," and the world began to drown.

While this was happening, the ark of Noah was floating above the water, saving the lives of those inside. Genesis 8:13–17 explains that after one year God spoke to Noah to go forth of the ark with his families and animals and multiply. All other life, it is said, was destroyed, and the earth was submerged for nearly one year.

After such a long flood, how could the dove find an olive branch while the water was receding? Most vegetation, I'm sure, was totally devastated and the animals released from the ark had no prey on which to live. Noah did not know ahead of time how long the Flood would last. There is a big question to be asked: "Where did he get the food supply for one year to feed all the animals?" Upon the release of Noah's menagerie, what did they all live on? Noah built an altar unto the Lord and took of every clean beast and fowl for a burnt offering to God.

The sweet savour stirred the Lord's heart and He promised never again to curse the ground for men's sake; neither would He again smite anymore everything living as He had done. This God is giving us the impression of repentance of His destructive ways and maybe will constrain His turbulent nature. Now you must search your heart again and decide if the God of Noah who drowned the whole world in His temper was an act of Love.

Moses was a shepherd, and while tending his flock on the Mount Horeb, the angel of the Lord appeared unto him in a flame of fire out of the midst of a bush. He looked in awe and beheld that the bush was afire but not consumed. The Lord called from the midst of the bush unto Moses and said, "Moses," and he answered, "Here I am," and the Lord arranged for Moses to see Pharaoh together with his brother Aaron as the spokesman. The Lord introduced Himself as the God of Abraham, of Isaac, and of Jacob, but they knew Him not as Jehovah! It came to pass that Moses and Aaron were often sent to Pharaoh by Jehovah and were rebuked by him every time. Their mission was to persuade the king to allow the people of Israel to go into the wilderness and bring offerings to their God. Every time Moses demonstrated the tricks that God gave him, Pharaoh was able to duplicate the same with his magicians and sorcerers, but the king was not impressed.

Finally, the Lord God told the Israelis to prepare for the passover, and that was when the Lord decided to kill all the first-born of men and of the beasts in Egypt. When the king and his people rose in the night and saw what had happened, he hastened to call Moses and Aaron and told them to take the people and go. It came to pass that the children of Israel journeyed from Ramses to Succoth on foot. The group consisted of about 600,000 adults, plus the children. Why did Jehovah kill all the first-born children who were innocent of the cause? If He possessed such power, why didn't He confound Pharaoh Himself to let the people go? Was the above action to kill all the first-born of Egypt an act of Love?

When the people of Israel left, they were promised by God that they would be led to the land of milk and honey. In the following verses, we are getting a good description of how that plan was supposed to work. Exodus 23:20–30 states: "Behold, I send an angel before thee, to keep thee in the Way, and to bring thee into the place which I have prepared." Verse 27 says: "I will send my fear before thee, and will make all thine enemies turn their backs unto thee." Verse 28 continues: "And I will send hornets before thee, which shall drive out the Hivite, the Canaanite, and the Hittite, from before thee." And in verse 30: "Little by little I will drive them out from before thee, until thou be increased, and inherit the land." The above plan of Jehovah was the beginning of the killings and wars to take other people's land for themselves and has been demonstrated throughout the Old Testament. Do you

127

consider chasing the people from their homes and lands by force an act of Love?

God saw Moses on Mount Sinai for forty days (Exod. 31:18), and the Lord gave unto Moses the testimony and the Ten Commandments written into two stone tablets. Upon his return to his people from the Mount of God, it came to pass that he saw them worshiping the golden calf. Moses's anger waxed hot; he cast the stone tablets from him and they broke. In Exodus 32:20, he took the calf they had made and threw it into the fire. Then he ground it into some water and made the people drink it. In 32:26, it states: "Then Moses stood in the gate of the camp and said, 'Who is on the Lord's side? Let him come unto me.' And all the sons of Levi gathered themselves together unto him."

The next verses continue: "And He said unto them, 'Thus saith the Lord God of Israel: Put every man his sword by his side, and go in and out from gate to gate throughout the camp, and slay every man his brother, and every man his companion, and every man his neighbor.' And the children of Levi did according to the word of Moses: and there fell of the people that day about three thousand men." Think about the freedom of religion today because the people of Moses had no choice except death. Shortly before this slaughter, Moses was carrying the Ten Commandments under his arm, including, "Ye shall not kill," but he was the first one to break them all. What about such mass murder? Is it an act of love?

In Numbers 5:1–4, we read: "And the Lord spake unto Moses saying, 'Command the children of Israel, that they put out of the camp every leper, and everyone that has an issue, and whosoever is defiled by the dead: Both male and female shall ye put them, without the camp shall ye put them: that they defile not their camps, in the midst of whereof I dwell.'" And they did as commanded. This God refused to dwell among the sick people, but I wish to remind you that Jesus healed them. Why wouldn't God do the same? Was this action Love?

Numbers 31:1–54 states: "The Lord spake unto Moses saying, 'Avenge the children of Israel of the Midianites.' " Verse 3 says: "And Moses spake unto the people saying, 'Arm some of yourselves unto the war, and let them go against the Midianites, and avenge the Lord of Midian.' " Moses ordered 12,000 men be armed for war and they warred and slew all the males and the king of Midian. In verse 9, the soldiers took some of the women and children captive and seized all the spoils of cattle and goods. They burned the cities and castles wherein they dwelled and brought all the spoils and captives unto Moses and Eleazar the priest and their congregation in the plains of Moab.

Verse 14 says: "And Moses was wroth with the officers and the captains, and said unto them, 'Have ye saved all the women alive?' " These caused the people of Israel to trespass against the Lord. Verse 17 reads: " Now, therefore kill every male among the little ones, and kill every woman, but only the virgin girls keep alive for yourself."

Can anyone imagine the horror awaiting those women and children and those virgins having to witness the fate of their loved ones? With the above slaughter of innocent and defenceless women and children, Moses fulfilled another commandment of his Lord. In verses 48 to 50, the officers and the captains counted the soldiers and reported that not one was missing, therefore bringing into the treasury of God an extra oblation of their loot to make an atonement unto the Lord. It is worthwhile to mention here that if not one soldier was unaccounted for, then that means the Midianites were not fighting. It is inconceivable that thousands of warring soldiers fighting in close combat against each other would really have on one side no loss of life. However, there would be an explanation if the so-called enemy was unarmed or surrendered. This cold-blooded murder of women and children leaves me numb. Was it a godly act of Love?

When the warrior life of Moses ended, Joshua was already in place to take over. He, too, was a great warrior for his God Jehovah. His most famous glory was Jericho. Joshua 6:1 explains that the city was surrounded by the soldiers of Israel and the Lord said unto Joshua, "I have given you Jericho, the king and its mighty men of valour." He gave them the strategy of conquering the city, and that all therein shall be a curse to the Lord.

In verse 17, only Rahab the harlot and her family and spies shall be saved, but all the silver and gold and vessels and iron are consecrated into the Lord and shall come into His treasury. It came to pass when the priests blew their trumpets and the people made a great shout, that the walls fell down flat and they took the city.

Verse 21 divulges that they totally destroyed all that was in the city, both men and women, young and old, and all animals were killed with the sword. They saved only the harlot and the spies, the silver, gold, vessels of brass and iron, which were taken into treasury of the Lord. The city was totally destroyed by fire, which fulfilled the famous commandment of Joshua for his God Jehovah.

Jericho: was this an action of Love? This concludes the short journey to the gods of the times. There are hundreds more of such examples in the Old Testament, but after reading a handful as outlined above, I cannot stomach more from these "masters of darkness." Those "horrid gods" of the times had no Love in their hearts. They only planted the seeds of evil throughout their history and were the kings of the worldly spirit. Whatever they were, or wherever they came from, they were imposters and pretenders of creation and did not possess the Holy Spirit of the God of Love.

16

Gods around the World

The jealousy demonstrated by Jehovah does not fit the God of Love, but rather compares to a worldly tyrant in our perception of today. To the people of Israel, he commanded, "Ye shall have no gods before me." When he gave Moses the order to kill all women and children, Moses said they were guilty because he claimed they caused trespass against the Lord. During those warring, biblical times, all the surrounding tribes, or so it seemed, were worshiping Baal, apparently with sufficient idols for every day of the year. What is missing here is the description of the spiritual value those idols stood for, because that alone will determine the inspirations those people received, and whether they were beneficial to their society. Just to love a god day and night because he is demanding it is the equivalent of a dictator, who is only using his devotees for his selfish purposes. There is a book full of evidence that the Israelites were nothing but pawns of the God Jehovah and that he manipulated their lives throughout the biblical times.

In the absence of Moses of only forty days, the people worshiped the golden calf. It seems so absurd that their belief in Jehovah was so shallow that all of them trespassed against him within only a few days! Even Aaron, the spokesman for Moses, did not have enough conviction to keep the people on the path of Jehovah, and he was the one who made the golden calf for them. Again we have to ask, why had they agreed for this idol and what was the mystifying spirit behind it? I have read it was associated with the spirit of fertility. If that is true, it definitely would play a large part in their lives on this earth because everything depends on this principle. Who knows, their idol worshiping might have turned out to be helpful for them, but instead, upon Moses's return, three thousand were killed because of this.

Jehovah's revenge to idol worshipers does not really make sense because he asked the same thing from Moses, that he build a tabernacle with handcrafted designs, cherubims, and angels. The ark, a very complicated enshrinement, was also built from the order of Jehovah. These are all idols to reckon with. Every shape and form portraying a godly function is an idol to that spirit or god; by it, you recognize and pursue your spiritual belief. There is no religion, cult or sect out there which does not have an amulet, a cross or a ring, a candle or incense, an altar or figurines, sculptures and statues of saints and gods. Those are all idols representing the spirit of the gods. We are all guilty of idolism and symbolism in describing our sensual feelings of the worldly spirit. I see nothing wrong with descriptions of idols as long as the spirit behind the idol portrays spiritual love.

That is where religion miserably failed. Just look at the Spaniards and other Europeans when they conquered America. They came with their flags, Christian religion, and guns, and people were murdered because of the precious necklaces they wore. Galleons upon galleons full of such gold and valuables were sent back to their kingdoms. In their eyes, natives were not yet humans. They could be slaughtered, used, and abused for what they had to offer. They brought their church with them to teach Christianity to the people they called heathen, and to destroy for whatever their beliefs might have been.

During those tumultuous centuries, I am sure those

Christian conquerors did not have their God with them but had probably left him behind in Europe! If it were not so, we would promptly have to ask, "Where was He during those massacres?" This brings us to the big question—yes, I am asking again—"Where was He?" There is no doubt in my mind that the God of Love was not in their hearts nor in their souls, but they were the walking death itself. Those were the clones of the Lucifers waving their banner of Christ before them to overcome the unwary by deception. That is the legacy in pictures and words in our history books.

The world is full of unsavory mischief wherever we look; nothing seems to change for the better since wars and famine are still with us. What must be done, or can be done, to break this evil spell of the worldly spirits? I reveal the answer, and it will bring hope to the world if they will heed the call to the "Philosophy of Love."

Beliefs of state religion were never a matter of individual choice, no, not even today. Countries of religious dictatorship are still exercising brutality against nonconformists. They have reached the pinnacle of self-glorification to the extent that they have reserved a first place in heaven for their heroes fighting the so-called holy wars. Who are these religious princes who exercise such authority over the heavens, and who needs a god if those imposters have a key over His domain? At least they pretend they have! A great multitude believe in their shrouded holiness, but, oh, this fragile curtain is only hanging on threads. The time is not far off when truth will make them fall and expose their Satanism. Their wisdom of yesteryears has served the medieval consciousness of mankind.

Science, for example, has scrambled itself loose from the Dark Ages and has excelled into exploring space, whereas religion has locked itself into a circle of its own righteousness of never changing or renewing its old-fashioned wisdom.

People of this world would love to live in countries with a higher standard of morality, but unless someone is teaching it, we cannot achieve it. The spiritual mixing bowl is the key for humanity to achieve such a goal, and the sooner it is taught the better, so that people will have another chance to live in peace on our planet. The Philosophy of Love is the manifestation of the Holy Spirit, and every living soul participating and teaching it will be His companion eternally.

Ancient Greece had many gods, and one of great importance was Apollo. Worship of this god was introduced into Greece from Asia Minor during the Dark Ages, about 1100 B.C. He was known as the dreadful god of prophecy. It was not until the sixth century B.C. that this god was associated with the arts, and the frightening aspect of Apollo was simmered down to mold him into the changing times. The people of Greece had gods and goddesses to comply with every occasion. It is interesting to note that all their gods were portrayed in human statues because during those ages, they did not perceive God as we do today in the divinity of the Holy Spirit. In approximately 300 B.C., a change of religion marked a trend toward Oriental cults based largely on magic and astrology. The schools of Plato and Aristotle were challenged by the appeal of epicurianism and stoicism, which had a great influence on Roman culture.

Egypt was the main centre in which the concept of the Sun God Ra was practised. A divine kingdom was determined by this solar deity. The pharaohs were considered the descendants or the incarnation of the sun god. This sun religion spread to the Orient and Europe by the way of the Romans and was considered unconquerable by them. Alexander the Great, because of his might and success as a warrior, was received as a god and celebrated by them.

There was no difference in the tribes that roamed the hills, the valleys and the desert regions of the Middle East and Arabia during those times. They, too, claimed that God was walking and talking with them, and all the prophets, seers, and astrologers were consulted by their kings. For example, the gods walked in the Garden of Eden, Abraham met two angels and the Lord in the plains of Mamre, and Jehovah was a god of the times strictly for the tribes of Israel in that region. It is demonstrated throughout the Old Testament that Jehovah was a warrior god—a dreadful one, similar to Apollo. They were not gods of love as we are visualizing today; they ruled and demanded love or be killed by the sword or pestilence. Fear was the motive, and those who still tremble from the threats are preaching of hell fire and brimstone until this day. They will remain slaves of fear until they realize that love is passing them by and that God is not found in the talents of man.

Thousands of different tribes throughout the world were strictly sectarian in their beliefs, each one proclaiming their god to be the only truth, and many went to extreme fanatacism to kill for him at a moment's notice. We all remember the horror of Jonestown where their high priest masqueraded as a Christian, and this happened only a few years ago. This living devil gave the order to commit genocide with poison, and it appeared they all complied with this horrible end. Those people, including children, walked into the trap of hell because they ignored the occurring evil symptoms. They could not use their free will because they had given it to the cult by joining. That is why I stress that all the people of this world should use the spiritual mixing bowl to determine for themselves if they are dealing with an unscrupulous deception of evil or if they are being confronted with Love.

In this day and age, we must have our feelers working because it is all too common that people of trust are abusing their positions. Newspapers are full of articles that we cannot ignore any longer about doctors to labourers, nuns to the

135

clergy, business people to politicians, law-enforcement officers to the highest position of judges, portraying the betrayal of the innocent. What possible reason can there be in our highly educated society for us to not have reached an acceptable moral standard? We can point our finger in only one direction—religion has failed humanity miserably because it does not teach the Philosophy of Love. If more politicians would be influenced by the teaching of Love then they would not loot the country's treasury. Instead, they would prefer to work for the people who elected them. The constitution of the land would read only the Philosophy of Love which contains all; there is nothing missing for our life's demands because all the needs and justice will be attainable by its use.

Whatever gods the whole empire of Alexander the Great, including Europe, adored up until the Middle Ages failed to influence the people with Love. They created hell on earth, and we must free our shackles from them. These gods of the times left no seeds of Love for us. Their seeds of fear have given us wars, famine, pestilence and sickness until this very day. Having talked about the influence of the man-made gods of the Middle Eastern regions, I feel we should acquaint ourselves with what kind of gods appeared in other parts of the world during these ages. How did the isolated people fare in the regions of China, while the Dark Ages of the bloodthirsty tribes and empires of the Middle East were passing by?

Throughout the ages of China, the Chinese people's philosophies and gods were not harnessed into an institution like religion. Their society was family-oriented and, to my surprise, women were the masters of the household. The Chinese believed that women had more influence with prayer and therefore had more effect than the menfolk. It was very interesting to learn about this attitude toward women because in other parts of the world they were no more than chattels to men. Various philosophers influenced the people of this most populated region of the world.

Confucius is one of the better known philosophers of China who was born into a noble family in 551 B.C. He began schooling at a young age and distinguished himself very early in life with spiritual qualities and modesty. Confucius taught that respect of the family was the all-important principle in everyday living. He said that human nature must be developed and refined by study and experience. The aim of his doctrine was to teach human beings to achieve fulness in life, by practicing the virtues of love. He hoped this endeavor would establish a high morality standard in the land. It was his belief that the reading of good literature would enhance intelligence and he strongly believed that by doing so, his people would be able to eliminate poverty.

The lifestyle amongst those people must have been very genteel in comparison to other parts of the warring world who displayed nothing but greed and power. Confucius's doctrine also supported the influence of ancestral spirits where each family conducted their own rites in honoring and appeasing them. He told the people to respect their government and that, in turn, they could expect justice for all. I am somewhat disappointed that the influence of the spiritual soul was not advocated, or maybe they didn't have the knowledge of it during that time. We cannot ignore reality, and to overcome worldly extremes we need the subtle influence from within, to learn that harmony will be the outcome in the balancing of our body and soul and in observing the virtues of Love.

Chinese history relates that in the year 2,752 B.C. the greatest of all Chinese wise men was born. Emperor Fohi was considered the supreme deity, the God of all mankind. He is said to be the reincarnation of the Holy Spirit, and they claimed he was born of a virgin without the ways of man.

Fohi is also lauded in Chinese history as being the first educator of the written Chinese characters. It is evident that during those ages the Chinese population was the most civil and moral people in the world.

Astrology was practiced in China since the earliest of times, and was studied for the sole purpose of astrological predictions. It was most important for an emperor to have this knowledge because the people had great faith in such a forecast. In the year 2,513 B.C. Emperor Chueni outlined the motions of the five planets. The chosen emperors were great masters in astrological knowledge and their wisdom was not connected with other parts of the world.

In 700 B.C. Lao-Tzu was born. He, too, was considered a reborn master from the year 1,321 B.C. His teachings were the concept of respect and love closely resembling spiritual Love. He was the author of the book *Tao-te-Ching* (supreme reason and virtue). However, it was said that his doctrine in later years became distorted because of the teachings of Taoism. These, apparently, had corrupted practices connected with magic and superstition.

In the year A.D. 1213 China came under the influence of Mongolia by the conquest of the Genghis Khan empire. They, too, were under the influence of a highly developed standard of astronomical and astrological proficiency. The mother of this legendary figure is also acclaimed with a virgin birth, and if this account is true it could certainly be acclaimed as the most dramatic of such a birth. His mother, a widow, became pregnant, which was against the law of the land, and when called before the chief judge of the tribe she declared that a blinding light had appeared in her room and had penetrated her body three times. She said she believed this to mean that she would bring three sons into the world, and if this did not happen then she would willingly submit to the established punishments. However, it did come to pass that she bore three sons and because of it she was then regarded as a saint. When Genghis Khan was born, the astrologist declared that a divine man had come into this world. The sign of Libra indicated that he would grow into an extraordinary genius and that he, too, would be well trained in astrology. It has been said that in the middle of his conquest of China he noticed the unfavorable alignment of the planets in his horoscope. These readings proclaimed doom, so he decided to head for home. Shortly after his arrival he died, at the age of sixty-five years.

The foregoing descriptions of other virgin births around this world might be interesting for Christians to read because they are convinced that this happened only to Mary and Joseph. The gods of the Mongols derived from their powerful influence of astrology that the sun, moon and stars were their guiding lights. For thousands of years, this science influenced their part of the world towards high moral standards. This gradually changed in Asia when the influences from Asia Minor, Arabia, and Europe took a foothold in their religions, politics and culture of the people of China. They welcomed various religions into their land in order to quicken the educational standard they desired. Before the time of Genghis Khan, Mongolians had no written language of their own, nor did they display a past history of their land. This was due to the high secrecy of burial methods demanded for their kings. They would choose a flat land for convenience, where all their favorite belongings would be buried with them, including an unknown number of virgin girls. Upon the completion of this event, this ground would then be trampled with hundreds of horses, erasing all traces of a burial site. To make sure that no one would find the location again, they killed all the grave diggers for good measure.

The Khan dynasty was the largest empire ever, and

lasted for almost two hundred years. This was probably one of the greatest cultural and trading integrations between nations of that time which advanced mankind a step nearer to racial and moral obligations. The records show that the Mongols, also, were barbarous warriors but they gave their victims a period of grace. They sent a delegation to a country they intended to conquer; but if they refused to surrender to their emperor, his armies would then utterly destroy that land.

On the shores of Japan the Imperial deity was Amaterasu, the sun goddess. They believed their first human emperor was a descendant from this celestial deity. This honor was still bestowed upon the recent Emperor Hirohito in 1926. At the time of his accession, he was officially considered a direct descendant of Amaterasu and therefore became a deity himself. However, after the Second World War, Hirohito was stripped of his divinity, but was allowed to continue as emperor of Japan.

The high abodes of towering peaks are another realm of various gods. They are the places where the rivers begin to flow and their waters are the life-blood of nature. Its moisture rises to form the clouds and will again return as rain, nourishing and washing clean once again the face of the earth. We drink it and are even made of it; we bathe in it and float in the gatherings we call rivers out to sea. This is the final home of all the waters we have seen and experienced as rain and snow, and we have enjoyed its wonders, greatness and beauty. Here is the place where all the power and glory of the water is concentrated; this is a place of miracles and recreation. Endless waves cause currents and process this power to make changes in the geography of continents.

Is it any wonder that out of the spirit of waters many gods were made to its glory by man? In the highest regions of the snow-capped mountains where the clouds enshrine the peaks is the holiest of places for the rain gods. Their abode is venerated all around the world because the worshippers believe it brings them closer to the God of gods, who is assumed to reside in those heavens above. The Old Testament tells us that Moses visited his God atop Mount Sinai; likewise, the Himalayan regions are considered equally important places. Along the Ganges River are the favored places for the reclusive holy men of India and for building caves and ashrams. The waters of the Ganges are considered holy—even today this region is as popular as it was in ancient times. Today the swamis have developed a meditation industry to cover the world with their wisdom in the regeneration of the sensual mind of the worldly spirit.

There are many more mountains venerated to gods and goddesses throughout Europe, Africa, and Asia. In the high regions of the Americas, we find similar evidence of high mountain worshiping places to various gods. Central America and the Andes Mountains are teeming with ruins, pyramids, and caves at high elevations.

Returning to the element of water, we are aware of its forces and its necessity for life on earth, thus it is not unreasonable to believe that it was, and still is, considered a great spirit of the cosmic power. All over the world, religious ceremonies are conducted with the use of water. Baptism is one example, where the person is immersed in water and comes up sanctified, and the sprinkling of holy water is another. In many places of the world, healing water, such as Lourdes in France, as well as hot springs and various mineral spas have been said to have curative powers for various ailments and that there is no end to its benefits. Those nations and tribes that pay homage to the sun and the moon as deities appreciate the various spirits of the water even more so because of the direct involvement of their gods. The sun is warming the waters, causing the moisture to rise and forming the clouds for the rain gods. The moon, on the other hand, will cool the waters at night and cause the tides of the seas. The food supply in the oceans seem endless, from the smallest of crustacea to the largest of whales.

There is also wickedness in its power when the fury of its spirit rolls a tidal wave to drown all the low-lying lands in its wake. This can be the cause of casualties and devastation never seen before. Swollen rivers can roar like unrestrained monsters howling along canyons and damaging bridges and anything in its path, and a new deity may be born again by those who live along its banks. The great deluge caused by the flooding of the world as written in the Scriptures, is surely a reason for mankind to pray for mercy to the rain gods that such catastrophes can be averted in the future. On all continents of the world, wherever the life-giving raindrops fertilize the earth, man, and beast, cultic acts have glorified the rain gods and their associated spirits ever since. Some holified the waters to the extreme in comparison to the understanding we have of water and its uses today.

For example, during the time of Genghis Khan, the religion of the Mongol tribes in the thirteenth century A.D. still forbade them to wash themselves, their clothes or their utensils with water because it was considered sacred and had to be kept pure. The ideology of keeping the water pure should be reintroduced into all countries of the world again in order to stop pollution without, of course, the sacredness of the Khan dynasty!

Having familiarized ourselves with some of the gods of Asia, what happened in the faraway Americas during those ages? Much of its history was destroyed by the European conquerors, but in the last century, great archaeological finds have been made. It is worthwhile to mention the efforts of Erich Von Däniken. The writings in his books have supplied us with enormous knowledge of artifacts from all over the world. He especially brings to light the ancient cultures of Central and South America, with his extensive explorations of caves and ruins, and of old temples and pyramids dating back into history that are on par with the pyramids of Egypt.

This part of the world seems to hide a past every bit as fascinating as anywhere else on this globe. It, too, had gods from faraway places or from the stars resembling many descriptions of the Old Testament and of Egypt. In Peru the ruling Inca was believed to be the sun incarnate (INTI) and his wife, the moon. A sun temple in Cuzco contains a representation of this first ruler as the oldest son of the Creator. The Indians in Central America called their king "Great Sun," and noblemen were called the "Suns." The sun was worshiped as male, in other areas of the world as female, and in some as a divine pair (*Encyclopaedia Britannica*).

Those similarities are surprisingly found wherever humanity flourished. The most hideous of all rituals must surely have been the human sacrifices that many gods demanded, for whatever reason, that such horrendous appeasements had to occur. Such rituals were looked upon as being a necessity of life. The Aztecs of Mexico fought battles to capture men as slaves to use as needed for human sacrifices, their god being insatiable. In their ancient annals, they tell us that twenty thousand prisoners were slaughtered for the inauguration of the great temple of Teocali. To some people, they say, it was an honour to be sacrificed to the gods, but there were never sufficient volunteers to appease the gods. They speak of quite a few of their deities in succession: Tezcatlipoca, Quetzalcoatl, Tlaloc, Quatlicue (goddess of the waters), and there were rain gods and fire gods as well. At the time of the Spanish conquest, the sun god was in control of the region of Mexico.

I am quite certain that in very ancient times sacrifices happened in many places. As a matter of fact, the Bible refers to sacrifices quite frequently. Abraham was asked by his god to sacrifice his only son, Isaac. He tied Isaac to the pile of wood and was about to start the ritual killing of his son when, at the last moment, an angel appeared with a lamb to be sacrificed instead. This is evidence that such sacrifices did occur because Abraham was a willing subject and knew exactly how to go about it in order to appease his god. Those horrendous burnt offerings varied in methods, purpose, and ritual. It appears that mankind was passing through phases of tribulation of self-imposed martyrdom because the worldly spirit was his only guidance.

I would like to believe that higher educational standards around the world would obliterate the barbarism that was practised during the Dark Ages. You would think that people educated in higher schooling, especially the ones indoctrinated in various religious beliefs, would find the answer to a more harmonious lifestyle in this world. Why has this not happened? If we look around this world of ours, we find countries such as Yugoslavia dotted with churches, so how can its citizens turn totally savage regardless of their education? In Ireland, for example, a religious guerrilla war has been brewing for decades, and very religious Middle Eastern countries continue to kill opposing factions, mainly for religious reasons. In Somalia, the rulers couldn't care less about the millions of people that are dying of hunger, and India also has religious problems; there is no end to dissatisfaction.

What is wrong? Is it the people or is it the gods who are causing continuous turmoil among living souls? Religion is afraid, or it doesn't know how, to ask God, and the people are afraid to ask religion because they are forbidden to do so; therefore, nothing ever changes. I truly believe that rot and stagnation have corroded the spiritual value of most doctrines preached from the pulpits. Preachers do not recognize

144

that the Holy Spirit is a continuous and renewed vitality and that it has knowledge that must be fostered by us.

It must be understood that our soul needs the companionship and wisdom from the Holy Spirit as a way of life in every hour of our existence. Some like to chase the rainbows around the world because a miracle happened here or there to someone. I say it again: it is the birthright of every living soul to partake of this divine flow. "Ask and you shall receive" is written in the book of heaven, and it does come to pass no matter if we are rich or poor, young or old.

Prestigious religious people think of themselves as the favorites of their gods, but such attitudes are immature and selfish, because only love is a factor. All religions believe that their deity is the creator of all things, the reason being that they all proclaim that He is the only true god amongst all other gods. If we take the evidence of all who walked and talked amongst the people, and those who appeared and disappeared on flying machines or clouds, we see that they are imposters. I call them the fallen angels and self-styled gods of the worldly spirit. It is that spirit that has taken over our worldly senses and befuddled the human mind into believing that the Creator was a duality of good and evil. Remember, Jesus said, "Ye cannot serve God and Mammon alike."

If you are called a Christian, then why would you believe in gods who gave orders or wantonly killed by themselves? What about gods with human traits of jealousy and revenge, or a god who condemned the lepers instead of healing them? I could go on and on, but not one of those gods had the divine flow of the Holy Spirit because that Spirit told me, quite emphatically, that no evil has ever passed through its messages and actions. I have submitted to relay this simple message so that we can close the curtain on the evil past of history behind us and step into the light of the living. We must redeem the spiritual mixing bowl to enable us to resurrect our soul and start into the new era of the Philosophy of Love.

This new philosophy is the "great divide" between good and evil. On the account of ignorance and greed, we wallow in pollution and experience a low morality standard, which is affecting all institutions of the countries in this world. The toleration of insurrection and wars to gain power and economic progress is still widely pursued. This ancient method has been used by barbarians for thousands of years. Such workings are of Satan and mark the evil side of the great divide. We must overcome those evil afflictions by initiating and pursuing the Philosophy of Love. On this good side of the divide, we will have hope for prosperity and finally peace because of inspirations from the Holy Spirit.

17

Astrology

Astrology was surely the first institution of mankind before any other kind of ideals became acceptable to his inquisitive mind. Lifestyles of nomad tribes showed that even the simplest of minds were able to associate the great importance of the sun, the moon, and the stars with his dependency on them. The heat and the rains would make things grow, possibly causing a variety of moods. Changes would continuously be induced with those forces by day and by night. During his sleep, the stars and the moon have their way upon his behavior for the next day to come.

It is, therefore, no wonder that thousands of years ago those influences were the beginning of education and higher learning for mankind. There were always those with quicker imaginations and desires who became attuned to the spirit of those worldly inspirations. Since then, gods were born for every occasion. The sun, moon, stars, birds, animals, men, and idols of all kinds had their times and ages as gods to man according to the evolutionary mentality.

Astrology is a living testimony to the established laws of God and of nature if correctly interpreted. If we realize that God created all things, then it is not hard to understand that most of the universal laws that regulate life and nature on this planet of ours, are caused by the Sun, the Moon, and the stars. They generate, for all mortal life, the energy that keeps us ticking. Only spiritual quickening can bring about the power to change this clock of life to move in a new direction.

This could be called the path of grace, which carries the power to overcome all evil. All miracles that have ever happened, all inspirations ever perceived, spiritual love and paranormal phenomenons are passed to us through this vibratory level. God's library is an open book, reachable by anyone with understanding and the ability to categorize with the intelligentsia of our free will. Let no man put a dogmatic barrier in front of the free will or beguile your inspired opinion lest you willingly renounce your free status and submit yourself to mental slavery.

Properly practised, astrology may contain the mystery we are faced to solve tomorrow not derived by any other means of science. It was most likely the first step of inquiry and the beginning of education for mankind. During its application, people have discovered, among other things, the period of a person's susceptibility to sickness and disease, therefore allowing them a calculated time to remedy or to counteract their derived prediction. Such knowledge was very important to people, especially to those in medicine, and this study has evolved into what we call today medical science. We cannot refute the influence of the motions of the heavenly bodies toward life on Earth; therefore denial of its importance can only explain ignorance of life.

It is the duty of human beings to explore all aspects internally and externally affecting our body and soul. I am aware that early church fathers referred to astrology as demon practises. Such a denouncement was a mere political ploy for self-gain, but it has damaged the respect of nature's hidden wisdom.

The obsession of mankind in deityfying at every opportunity has put the Holy Spirit into obscurity. We are idolizing everything from without, but we are ignoring the truth from within. Religion and astrology are two different institutions. From the latter we can derive knowledge essential for the body, health, and guidance of its revelation. No particular belief is needed to exploit its truth, whereas the former should be the inspiration of the soul and its doctrines based on faith alone. Both depend on the sincerity of their practitioners; otherwise they can be blamed equally for demonic practises. As the saying goes, "There is hardly a tree without a rotten apple on its branches." This is why I advocate the use of the spiritual mixing bowl because love must always be the outcome in our endeavors, no matter what we join or do. It will bless our hearts and keep us on the path of joy.

18

Instinct—the Worldly Rule

We are humbly aware that our sophisticated being must bend to every rule of nature and that we are regulated and subjected by the forces of the Sun, the Moon, and the stars. The influence of our planet by these forces has truly established the perfect utopia for all living creatures and plant life on this Earth. The seasons come and go, and with them the great changes of all vegetation take place in front of our eyes. The leaves begin to fall and the flora starts to wilt—it seems as though everything is dead by the time it snows.

Come spring, the miracle will start all over again; new life will come forth and everything will bloom once more. If we are blessed with long life, we can experience this process very often and therefore understand that the spirit of the root or bulb contains the code to grow again as beautiful as ever. Could we say that its soul survived during the long winter for another incarnation of its earthly life cycle? It has total dependency upon the wheel of nature, and it applies equally to all other animal life, including *Homo sapiens*. All sensual physical bodies of living creatures are guided according to their own code of instinct applied by the laws and principles of creation. It is not my belief that instinct has anything to do with a preordained destiny, but rather that it is the docile following of the code. That behavior will then determine the outcome of destiny for each living thing with one exception, man.

We are endowed with the free will and a higher intelligence than all other creatures; therefore, we ought to know about the existence of our spiritual soul and its purpose. This divine influence from within has to be determined by our free will and then applied to our determination of our worldly intentions. If this influence of Love is used in our daily lives, it would be the only power that is not in the jurisdiction of the solar system to influence us. With this advantage, we can change at will the direction that instinct is leading us, thereby becoming the master of our destiny under the laws and in the care of God. I have been told that without this power of Love given by the Holy Spirit, man can fall from holding human virtues to becoming the most wicked beast of hell.

Such monsters are visible all over the world, and it would be prudent for our courts to derive their punishment from the mundane justice, "Ye shall reap as sown." It seems fair to the spirit of the cosmos, and there is no distinction of age or sexes. For example, a wilful capital murderer has forsaken the code of being human and is reacting on instinct alone, therefore must suffer the consequences according to the beast. Religion will argue that the human form is the image of God, but in my opinion and experience, it is not the mortal image that deserves this comparison but the spiritual soul within. Is it not written that the breath of life entered the formed body and became a living soul? This process is repeated in the birth of every human being. Upon its first breath, it becomes an individual duality, and on its last breath, this bond is broken for the soul to be freed from its worldly cycle.

This divine law of birth and rebirth of the soul to experience life on this planet is not without purpose. The many failed missions of the soul are the direct result of false teaching and the insatiable excesses of our senses. In this accepted process of life, we are seldom content with our achievements:

the goal we wish to reach is moved from time to time to a more distant future for more and better things to come. Life, in the meantime, passes by in melancholy for so many and in fighting wars for others. Thousands still die of hunger because the fruits of man's worldly spirit and his mammon gods have vastly damaged the human code. Morality is at the low ebb, its standards are corrupted by deceit, and man's laws are crying out for justice.

The above is not a situation that surprised us overnight; this is the lifestyle chosen or enforced by our elite of kings, politicians, and religions. These are the institutions of the world that wield the stick of great power because of their sheer numbers. They have the influence in politics, business, and community life to change world affairs in a short time, especially now that television and news media are available twenty-four hours a day. Instead, they have chosen to keep a strangely inverted silence. Without fail, the newspapers are full of advertising to attract attendance at various churches, and some religious organizations take over the TV stations on weekends for live broadcasts and money collecting—but very rarely are such offerings donated to the hungry of the world.

Misconduct of their ministers has grown to epidemic proportions: some have taken vows of celibacy only to be caught in the molestation of children and others have committed adultery and embezzlement. The most disturbing fact is that these criminals are allowed to continue in the ministry, with their congregations accepting them back or allowing them to be moved to repeat their crime elsewhere. How can we condone such behavior, especially under the roof they call the house of God? They bring forth the excuse that we must learn to forgive, heaven forbid, in such a case where people claim they had a calling. One criminal act is one too many and cannot be forgiven by any parishioner nor by the high in command. Such a man not only deceives the people who believed in him but also makes a mockery out of morality and betrays God on the sly.

Our worldly instinct comprises the physical attributes we can perceive, and every thought created by our brain and senses will be stored worldly memories. From all those sensual actions and thought processes, an accumulation of energy is emitted in the form of various moods. I call this lingering overflow the worldly spirit, what dreams are made of and when telepathy may be transmitted. Such inspirations and translations can mistakenly be interpreted as the Holy Spirit, but its messages will always determine the Truth. The above description will give my readers a small account of the worldly spirit as I experience and perceive it. It is important to realize that the latter is our dominant spirit and carrier of good and evil. In contrast, the Holy Spirit is the carrier of only good and its manifestations through our soul is Love.

I have been told that no man has ever received a message of evil substance from the Holy Spirit. This knowledge is of great significance—it will change the structure of all religious beliefs if the two separate spirits concept is understood. Mankind has suffered horrendously because of its ignorance, and it is my sincere hope that this new spiritual enlightenment will open eyes and minds to stop confusing the works of the God of Love with the evil tidings of the worldly spirit. When this happens a new spiritual era will rise and the hearts of man will begin to pray out of Love instead of fear. The evil curse written into history by the lords of duality, and still upheld by religious doctrines and glorified, must leave your mind and shatter into oblivion to make room for the Holy Spirit. This housecleaning in your heart and mind is essential, and the assurance of Jesus when He stated, "The temple of God is within" will help you to overcome evil.

It is not my intention to be discourteous to our renowned

churches of this world. I feel it was my privilege to join or study most of them. I would like it to be known that I have great admiration for the work they are doing in every community. The parishioners are satisfied with what they are taught, but when it comes to the subject involving God of Love and the Holy Spirit, the Truth has not yet surfaced.

In my message I will frequently mention the shortcomings of religion, especially of the Christian religions since I, myself am a Christian. Herein, let me apologize to all who feel my words are a trespass against them. It is not my intention to do so. Most people in the clergy profess to have a calling, and therefore I expect them to likewise respect mine. There are thousands of people, professional writers, who could have made a superb job of bringing this joyful message across to this world. Somehow the privilege fell on me . . . why? I am no writer, not without blemish and certainly nobody of importance. Perhaps I received this privilege because of my sincerity and persistence.

When I started this journey in earnest to look for, and to find, the God of Love, I never tired or abandoned my plans. There was always the drive and the need to know more. Religion and libraries became my focuses, and I often read into the night until the birds began to sing to proclaim another day for our blessing. Looking back, it is fair to say that I stomped through the religious jungle of man for forty years. This description is not unfair if we consider the thousands of religious organizations that are scattered everywhere, each one claiming to be the house of God, the Truth and nothing but the Truth. I was amazed to see hardly anyone unattached to one group or another. They all had similarities and needed the security of a church community. This belonging was more important than God Himself because they believed that attending church was sufficient to be in His grace. I was in the midst of those congregations, but my search was not of their concern and my heart was crying out, "Where are you, God of Love?"

I had a goal to prove or disprove in my heart, Is there, or is therc not a God of Love? And if there is, then where will I find this elusive God? Maybe some of you can now sympathize with me when I talk about the religious jungle of man. If you don't agree with me, then go out there amongst them and try to find the God of Love. Only when you hear from the pulpit that God is jealous and revengeful, handing out pestilence and brimstone—or other wickedness that is not of Love—will you know you are in the wrong place. It will finally dawn on you that Love and evil do not mix.

The question arises, "Does God possess and make use of both those specific differences?" If He does resort to evil deeds as described in the Old Testament, then calling Him "Love" would be a gross misquotation. A god, or king, or any other man for that matter who will issue an order to kill defenceless women and children is, in my mind, nothing more than a barbarous, heartless monster. We claim to live in a cultured society. How, then, can educated man continue to glorify gods and prophets guilty of such atrocities? Those were my concerns in my spiritual adventure. I found myself face to face with religions that condoned such practises committed by their holy men and the deities they adored. To my continued disappointment, everything I came across was serving only the worldly spirit.

Astrology is man's oldest science, religiously venerated by man for thousands of years. We cannot deny its direct influence on the human body and our worldly affairs. Countless gods were created in honor of those forces, influencing the mind and body all our lives. If mankind would have studied and understood them for what they were, and if their spirits were inspiring to living souls, they would have eventually understood their connection to God. There should be

155

no jealousy by Jehovah as described in the Bible because such interactions were the holiest of intentions.

Instead, evil inspirations by the worldly spirits led to great confusion between body and soul, neglecting the voice from within. Instinct had its way, and the free will was dormant when those spiritual dead commanded the world. They killed endless human beings and animals as sacrifices to appease the evil spirits conceived in their ignorance of darkness. Some of those bloodthirsty lords of good and evil are still entrenched in the dogmas of many religions, and until they vanish from our hearts and minds, we are not free to accept the God of Love.

Jesus was the first human being to bring into the world the Philosophy of Love. He said, "In Love all things are fulfilled," but unfortunately not even Christians understand this all-inclusive statement. They continue to glorify, but pay little attention to the above statement of Jesus for which He sacrificed His life. Until we start to honor and live under the principle and laws of that holy statement, His death will have been in vain. In that statement lies the secret and power of forgiven sins if we follow His way.

Declaring Him to be God despite His objections does not make a person a Christian. If we repent because of Him, we must also follow His commandments. There can be no forgiveness until we start on the road of compensation. That is why He continuously mentioned in His doctrine to follow Him and do the Will of His Father. Why would He stress this relentlessly if it wasn't all that important? So many preach from the pulpit to just accept Jesus in your heart right now and all will be forgiven. Is it really that simple to shed all your past evils, if there were any, or is this miracle they preach a mere temporary stunning ploy?

Evangelistic crusades have greatly honored themselves for spreading the wings of Christianity faster than ever around the world. There is no doubt that they draw enormous crowds and millions of listeners on radio and TV preaching the miracle above, because of His crucifixion. They miss out on a great opportunity to inform their congregation of the real cause of His doctrine, that we must live in the Philosophy of Love, which in Jesus's terms was the Will of God. The renowned worldly crusaders are the very elect of the churches—the ones with the "gift of the gab." I was told they are the religious stars of TV and radio, and while what they have to say might be negligible, how they say it is all-important to impress the crowds and listeners.

I have attended some evangelistic services myself. They do not vary much in content, and their most important messages are the promises they claim were made by Jesus. First, they say that our sins are already forgiven because of His crucifixion and, second, that nothing you give monetarily is too much for Jesus because you will get tenfold in return. Those two dandies are the trump cards to soften the people's hearts and wallets, which make those "stars of the pulpit" instant tycoons of the worldly spirit variety.

Many of them have been known for embezzling church funds, living high on the hog, and living adulterous lives. Many of those left are being checked by the government for possible tax evasion. What amazes me is that millions of people will forgive these cheats of their losses. I can assure you in the spirit of Jesus and His words that they are not forgiven; remember that He said they will pay to the last farthing. To collect money in God's and Jesus's name is, if you will pardon my expression, spiritual extortion. Money collected under those means cannot be excused except for the hungry of the world and the downtrodden; no other cause is justified to use God or Jesus as a collection box.

The world is full of Bible colleges where Christian missionaries and ministers of churches are studying the Gospel.

Why do they flip over, ignore or do not want to understand important messages of His teachings? For example, when a rich man confronted Jesus and told Him, "Master, I lived up to all the commandments. What else need I do to get into Heaven?" Jesus then told him, "Sell all you have and give it to the poor, and then follow me."

If you really study the advice of Jesus given to the man, it is obvious there is something very important missing in His message. Have you noticed that there is no mention to give ten percent to the church or to His own cause from the rich man's fortune? Take note, you spiritual tycoons: He did not ask for a single farthing for His ministry and even stressed to the apostles when they were preaching not to carry a script.

Commanding them not to carry a script on their way to deliver a sermon is somewhat mysterious because no minister today worth his salt would preach without one. I wish to enlarge on this important subject to find the reason for His objection to carrying a script. Those of you reading or studying the Bible must surely have found the answers to this puzzling question. If you recall, He was upset that so many of men's laws were in their holy books, as if they were God's laws.

Religion will argue that this was during the time of Jesus, but I am certain it has not changed much since, and His words would echo no differently now than in the past. Even though He quoted the text of Moses and the Ten Commandments, Jesus expected His apostles to preach the Word from within like He did with the inspirations from the Holy Spirit or as He mentioned so often, from His Father. He told us to do the same and promised that we, too, would be inspired if we followed His teachings. Reflecting into my past with joy, I recall taking His advice, and in the process, I had my soul resurrected to its rightful place. There is no written word that doesn't pass through the spiritual mixing bowl before my acceptance of its love and truth; free will was given to us for this very purpose.

Earlier on, I implied that Jesus was not God. This is not my own opinion but is from His own denials. Here, I present His statements. In John 14:10, He said, "Believest thou not that I am in the Father, and the Father in me? The words that I speak unto you I speak not myself: but the Father that dwelleth in me, he doeth the works." He continued in John 14:12: "Verily, verily, I say unto you, He that believeth on me, the works that I do shall he do also"; and greater works could be done by man than He accomplished.

It would be way out of line to hint at such a suggestion if He were God. It is also interesting to note in the epistle of the apostle Paul in Romans 8:14 that "for as many as are led by the Spirit of God, they are the sons of God." This, I presume, would clarify why Jesus is called the Son of God by mankind because He was inspired by the Holy Spirit, but He always referred to Himself as the son of man.

For good measure I will refer to one more verse. In Mark 10:18, it states: "And Jesus said unto him, Why callest thou me good? There is none good but one, that is God." When He said, "I and my Father are one," He tried to tell us that He was in complete harmony with the Word of God by whom He was inspired, but His intentions were never to consider Himself an equal to God. Those were total misconceptions by His followers who were oftentimes hard-pressed in deciphering the parables He spoke to them. It is no secret that the apostles did not even understand what Jesus meant for a long time when He spoke to them about the Father within and in heaven. They asked Jesus to show them the Father so that they could believe in Him also; this makes it quite clear that they were very much earthlings up to that time and were not yet inspired by the Holy Spirit.

Jesus proclaimed that He had overcome the world and that it was within every living soul to conquer the worldly spirit by having our soul resurrected from the spiritual dead. That brings us to the reference He made to one of His apostles when he asked permission to attend his father's funeral and Jesus answered him, "Let the dead bury the dead." In the worldly sense, we understand this to be impossible, but when He spoke of the dead, He meant what I just mentioned above. Then He attested that man must be born again.

In John 3:5–7, Jesus answered, "Verily, verily, I say unto thee, Except a man be born of water and the Spirit, he cannot enter the kingdom of God. That which is born of the flesh is flesh; and that which is born of the Spirit is Spirit. Marvel not that I said unto thee, Ye must be born again." In the above verses, He is referring to our body and soul. We need both to function as a harmonious duality in order to live the Word of God, which is manifested in the Philosophy of Love.

Without the resurrection of our dormant soul, we have no assurance of our free will; therefore, we are easy pickings for monetary prophets or for ending up as human tragedies like Jonestown. There are false prophets everywhere who are inspired by the worldly spirit of mammon. Some show you how to meditate for relaxation—at a price. Others will focus on concentration to obtain wealth—also for money—and others make you a monetary slave in selling flowers to cushion the guru tycoon with the pleasures of life. All the above constitute aberration of the worldly spirit and have no direct relationship whatsoever to the Holy Spirit. The same holds true for hundreds of cults and religious organizations the world over. If you are one of their members, use the spiritual mixing bowl. It will keep you informed if Love is always supreme or subdued, and if the temptations of the instinct have been overcome by the inspirations of the Holy Spirit.

19

Holy Places of Religion

The world is dotted with places of worship, and all have a holy sanctum or altars of special importance. Those places are decorated with figurines of gold to portray the sanctity of their Lord or God. The great splendour and riches must incense the most skeptical to the allure of their offerings. Millions of people travel to holy lands such as the Vatican, Mecca, the Himalayas, and Jerusalem, to name a few. What makes a person travel halfway around the world to see these places? Is it perhaps to have a feeling of closeness to God? Do people really believe that He is hiding out in these places, or is it that those places are created by man where God is realized according to the sweet offerings by them?

The Bible is full of variations of savourings to the Lord. He could smell their burning carcasses all the way into His abode, and it says He was pleased and honored as long as the offering was without blemish. There were special places for human sacrifices where the still-beating heart cut out of a person was held high in order to gain favor of a wrathful God.

On Mount Sinai God commanded Moses to build a sanctuary out of carved shittim wood, gold, silver, fine linen, brass, onyx stones, and carved stone plates, etc.—a list of craftsmanship, riches, and elegance. The elaborate tool-made assembly of this holy place covers the last five chapters of Exodus 35:40: Jehovah's demand for such glitter is a surprising and astounding change of taste. Upon the first meeting with God on Mount Sinai, He told Moses, in Exodus 20:25, "And if thou wilt make me an altar of stone, thou shalt not build it of hewn stone: for if thou lift up thy tool upon it, thou hast polluted it."

Those two amazingly different requests are so contradictory that the reader must surely wonder if that message came from the same God. Moses received both messages on Mount Sinai only a short time apart. It makes me wonder if his God was forgetful about tool-crafted pollution, or could it be that this God could not resist the glitter of gold they had brought from Egypt when they departed under His command? The glory of the second holy sanctuary was the beginning of tool-crafted holy places carried into this day, and we can all see with our own eyes the glory of the golden domes and spires reaching high into the sky.

Not only was the sanctuary of Moses a jewel of the times, it also exerted great power by its use. God gave Moses confidence to war around the area of Jericho and against the defenceless Midianites. Moses gave orders to kill all, but the reluctance of the soldiers saved the virgin girls—which they could keep as a token reward. The power of the holy sanctuary continued with Joshua who took Jericho and slew everyone, including women and children, and gave the order to save only the gold. If those stories are true, then we are safe to say that the savagery of World Wars I and II are nothing new but a repeat abuse of power in the name of God.

Holy places are man-made domains to glorify themselves in the accompaniment of the masses. It would be well for those Christians to read 1 Corinthians 3:16–17: "Know ye not that ye are the temple of God, and that the Spirit of God dwelleth in you? for the temple of God is holy, which temple ye are." According to Jesus there is only one holy place, and that is your spiritual soul within, which He calls the temple of God. It is so very close; pray, and you will become aware of it so that you are able to enjoy the holiest place on earth wherever you are.

20

Mind-Boggling Contradictions

Sometimes our work took us into small towns too far away to commute, so on such occasions, my business partner and I would spend the night in an available country inn. One evening, I noticed a book with the inscription "The Holy Bible" on the night table. When I took it into my hand, my partner asked, "Have you ever read this book?" "No," was my answer, "I have never read it before."

He seemed very knowledgeable about it, and during that evening, I became aware that he was a very religious man. After a couple of evenings together, it became apparent, and he told me so, that he believed every word in those Scriptures. At that time, I was a complete novice regarding the content, so whatever his convictions were, they were fine with me.

Later on, I tried to dispute some of his findings but was quickly put in my place when he said, "Having faith means believing every word in the Bible." He suggested that I read the end of the Bible, including Revelation 22:18, which says, "For I testify unto every man that heareth the words of the prophecy of this book, If any man shall add unto these things, God shall add unto him the plagues that are written in this book," plus I read about the punishment in verse 19. It could easily be seen that my religious friend was totally incensed by fear rather than by a teaching that should convey love.

Those vulgar threats in the end of the Bible they call holy are definitely very confusing.

Since those evenings took place in that country inn forty years have passed, but I have studied the Bible continuously ever since. The words of my friend are still with me when he stated that the Bible was compiled only by inspired men. It is unfortunate that he never knew of which spirit they were inspired because in the meantime, I can testify to two different spirits.

The worldly spirit is dominant in human beings. Its influence in worldly affairs and religion is enhanced by our educational system, which encourages greed and power. The god of this spirit is mammon, which carries no morality standard and is free to mess with good or evil relations. Excesses of any kind, broken promises by politicians, abuses of power, criminality and all religious doctrines opposed to love are but a few favorite inspirations of the worldly spirit. In summary, the worldly spirit is the carrier of good and evil as demonstrated for us throughout the Old Testament in the Bible. I hope that my description has made it clear that the human race is influenced and guided mainly by the worldly spirit.

The Holy Spirit, on the other hand, is the manifestation of Love, and mankind has never asked for its inspiration. Therefore, the soul is kept dormant and not used. This spirit carries only goodness and has never transmitted any evil in its communications or actions. This is the spirit religion pretends to have, but this is not taught in their dogmas. The Holy Spirit is there for us to use and to live in its manifestation, which is the Philosophy of Love. "Seek and ye shall find, knock and it shall be opened, ask and ye shall receive": these statements are the threshold to the Holy Spirit, and Love is the fulfillment of its influence.

The continuous confusion and misunderstanding of the

Holy Spirit has given room to greedy, wicked, and unsavoury abusers by the holy pretenders in this world. Listen to my trumpets—they herald loud and clear that if you are sincere in finding the God of Love, then I urge you to use the spiritual mixing bowl. Only then should you decide to join a religious organization, cult or guru. They might promise spirituality by the adherence to their dogmas or by a vegetarian diet. Food goes into your stomach, and it is definitely a personal health science of what is appealing and good for the physical body. All of us have various needs and eating habits whereby the worldly spirit may be affected. Our food selections and necessity thereof have absolutely nothing to do with the Holy Spirit—that I can testify in truth from my own soul.

In order to acquire the Holy Spirit, we must have the desire in our hearts; by this alone, the valve in the soul will open to inspirations of love. There is only one restriction to pursue the Philosophy of Love, and that is to abstain from evil actions. Remember, things are harmful to your health and soul if they clash with the virtues of love. These are the only guidelines to follow in pleasing the God of Love. Everything else is made up of rules and devious conceptions deliberately, or through ignorance, used in spinning a web to catch the unwary for the sake of mammon. My experiences of forty years have proven to my body and soul that the Holy Spirit is our birthright. The knowledge gained thereby will be righteousness, and the soul will be overflowing with joy.

My description of the foregoing, which is of two vastly different spirit phenomenas, must be fully understood by my readers in order to be prepared to comprehend so many contradictions in the Bible. My friend swore that every word written in it is true, but I feel that my readers should have the right to draw their own conclusions from this mess for themselves. The apostle James made it clear that his god is not being termed a tempter, and he has a lengthy explanation about temptation in his first chapter. I wish to narrow it down to verse 13: "Let no man say when he is tempted, I am tempted of God: For God cannot be tempted by evil, neither tempteth He any man." The gods of Eden tempted Adam and Eve by placing the Tree of Knowledge in the middle of the garden. They were told not to eat of its fruit, but they could not resist such a temptation for long.

The Lord God tempted Abraham, as explained in Genesis 22:1–16: "To sacrifice his beloved son Isaac at Jehovah-Jireh." This heartbreaking temptation was demanded by God in order for Abraham to prove his loyalty to Him. The charade raises another question because Jesus taught that God knows everything even before we ask. Why did this God not know the loyalty of Abraham and tempt this man to kill his beloved son at the stake?

The Book of Job refers to a very rich man who was perfect, upright, and who feared God. This man, it says, did no evil and lived with his family of seven sons and three daughters. In Job 1:1–22 and 2:1–13, there is a lengthy account of how the Lord conferred with the sons of God and amongst them was Satan. In order to prove to Satan Job's godly loyalty, God gave free reign to Satan to destroy all the man's possessions plus his children, but gave Satan the order to save the life of Job. I want you to read at least two chapters of this hellish collaboration between the so-called God and Satan. I don't know how you will interpret the command of God, which caused endless grief and death to Job's family. The destruction of his possessions was only to prove a point. I can tell you from my soul that the Holy Spirit had absolutely nothing to do with those masters of darkness.

We all know the great story of Jehovah who besought Moses with tricks to tempt Pharaoh to let the people go. To make a long story short, Moses's tricks did not work, so Jehovah took it upon himself to kill all the first-born of Egypt.

167

This is called the Passover, and it is a great celebration in some religions today. The temptation in this case did not work but ended in a slaughter of all the innocent first-born children. If Jehovah had all that power, could he not have confounded the mind of Pharaoh instead of causing this gruesome murder spree?

Moses was a murderer before Jehovah met him and between those two, blood was flowing like rivers until the death of Moses. Strange as it may seem, the day Moses was given the Ten Commandments, he gave the order to murder three thousand people. One of the commandments said: "Ye shall not kill," but this did not stop any one of those prophets and kings from killing in the name of God. In my heart those contradictions are definitely mind-boggling because there is no justification in all those senseless atrocities committed by them. Again, from the bottom of my soul, the God of Love had nothing to do with that hell-fire of the worldly spirit.

We are in conflict between the Old and the New Testament because of many statements made by the apostles. In 1 John 3:15, it reads: "A man cannot hate his brother without being a murderer, and you may be sure that no murderer has eternal life dwelling in him." This statement is telling us that there is no eternal life for murderers. If this is the belief of Christians, then we certainly cannot accept the prophets and the gods of the Old Testament as being true or holy. On this one I am definitely siding with John because the Philosophy of Love is a total stranger to the history of the Old Testament.

Those recycled warrior gods of old served only the kings and had nothing but contempt for humanity. In the New Testament it is demonstrated, and we are told, that evil functions are of the devil or Satan. For example, when Peter had a dispute with Jesus, He told Peter, "Get thee behind me, Satan" (Mark 8:33). If we choose to believe the wording of Jesus, then it is not difficult for Christians to classify the

168

evil-doings of the lords in the Old Testament. They were the gods of darkness and not of the God of Love.

21

Sequence of Creation—Tree of Knowledge

Christian religions swear by the Bible and tell us that everything in it is the truth and nothing but the truth, God-inspired, and holy. When I read the Bible for the first time I became stuck on the first page and read it at least ten times. There seemed to be a mixed-up sequence of Creation, which I am certain was not the way God created this earth of ours. Maybe the inspired writers had too much wine or had no idea of what influence our solar system has on our planet.

On the first day of Creation, God said, "Let there be light, and there was light, and God saw the light, that it was good: and God divided the light from the darkness, and God called the light day, and the darkness He called night." Why, then, was it necessary to create the Sun, the Moon, and the stars on the fourth day to give light to the Earth, as well as day and night, which apparently existed already since the first day? On the third day, God created grass, herbs, fruit trees, etc. Ironically, as you already know, God created the solar system on the fourth day. Have you asked yourself, "How could the vegetation grow without the sun?"

Why don't you ask God, as I did? The answer is, before the Sun, the Moon, and the stars, there was no soil, neither could vegetation grow without the laws of nature, which needs the Sun, the Moon, and the stars. So don't tell me again that everything in the Bible is the Truth and nothing but the Truth. I also rightfully claim that the gods of the times upon which religions were built were not of the God of Love I have found. Those gods of the Old Testament were void of Love. I wish to give you one more example to ponder, regarding written Truth. In Genesis 1:26–31, God created man, male and female, and God blessed them and said unto them, "Be fruitful and multiply," and God gave them dominion over everything, including all creeping and crawling things. At a later time, God commanded them, as stated in Genesis 2:17: "But of the tree of knowledge of good and evil, thou shalt not eat of it: for in the day that thou eatest thereof thou shalt surely die." But the snake, which was smarter than man, knew the Tree of Knowledge and had persuaded Eve to eat of its fruit, and so it came to pass that Adam and Eve knew they were naked. The story goes that they were punished by God, and the question remains: "Why?"

God blessed them to multiply long before this episode occurred, so how could it be accomplished without the Tree of Knowledge? And why would God give dominion to man to rule over a more superior species than himself? The snake, for example, was smarter than Eve—think about it! The way the whole story of Adam and Eve is presented has caused endless humiliation, inequality, segregation, and slavery for women since the time of the Garden of Eden. Throughout history, women were not allowed to work in the ministry of religion because of that episode.

The apostle Paul commented about women, and with his statement, he renewed the old stigma of discrimination! I find his declaration quite insulting and degrading for women everywhere. With today's strife over human rights, I would encourage the women's liberation movement to find the cause before fighting the symptoms of inequality. The

171

cause was religion the world over; the Garden of Eden was the beginning.

The people, especially those who call themselves Christians, should read what Apostle Paul had to declare about women in 1 Timothy 2:9–15:

> In like manner also, that women adorn themselves in modest apparel with shamefacedness and sobriety; not with braided hair, or gold, or pearls, or costly array; But [which becometh women professing godliness] with good works. Let the woman learn in silence, with all subjection. But I suffer not a woman to teach, nor to usurp authority over the man, but to be in silence. For Adam was first formed, then Eve. And Adam was not deceived, but the woman being deceived was in transgression. Notwithstanding she shall be saved in childbearing if they continue in faith and charity and holiness with sobriety.

I find the above verses entail more scorn than love. The seventh verse of Timothy with its description of woman is in stark contrast with the words about men in verse 8: "I will therefore that men pray every where, lifting up holy hands, without wrath and doubting." That is all he had to say about men. This is clear evidence that equality was not in the apostle's heart.

It is written that Adam did eat of the fruit as well and therefore was equally guilty, but only Eve was blamed and cursed, according to Genesis and religious rulers afterwards. The old tradition of keeping women in silence is beginning to frustrate the intellect of modern civilization with feelings of guilt and to acknowledge the injustice done. Women's liberation has found new hope in its endeavor and women are demanding equal rights worldwide. The Philosophy of Love knows no distinction between man and woman, and

God did make them equal. It is gratifying to see that equality has taken root and that justice may not be too far off.

The story is a typical fabrication of man's worldly spirit, and it is no longer taken seriously because modern man is not as gullible as he used to be. There is a time of reckoning of everything that transpires; Truth and Love will stand the test, whereas delusion has no foundation. God of Love does not care who was first formed, justice has no preference because of it, nor is the assumption of the transgression of Eve valid. Both Adam and Eve had been warned not to partake of the fruit; however, both did eat thereof. Therefore, love was not present when Eve received a harsher punishment than Adam, and Eve was also labeled the first sinner of mankind. This stigma attached to women was conceived by the early religious scribes. It must and will be undone by our churches once ministers preach the Philosophy of Love and receive inspirations from the Holy Spirit through their soul.

22

Finding the Way

The world has been hit by lightning! Its fires are burning, slowly decimating dictatorship and autocracy, which have governed civilizations for thousands of years. The scorn of the people toward such barbarous regimes is causing much uprising and change around the globe. The United Nations of today has finally reached a beginning of mutual understanding to speak and act in unison against such evil oppression. Hopefully in the future, they will successfully eliminate dictatorships from this planet.

Courageous people from all four corners of the world are demanding from their governments open dialogue, equality, free speech, free enterprise, religious freedom, and freedom to travel. Human rights and environmental concerns are the daily cards the governments have to deal with in ever-increasing demands. In such a climate, is it any wonder that this encourages free thinkers to inspire and reach for greater heights than ever before in every aspect of life? Better education will eventually lift man out of illiteracy and low self-esteem festered by past autocratic systems.

A beam of light is descending upon our civilization for the first time in our historic memory, heralding hope from the star of peace. Our past few decades have attested to many miraculous achievements because of free enterprise. Just mentioning the outer space program and the arrival of the computer age, there seems to be no limits for those entrepreneurs of visions to benefit mankind. Over the past one hundred years, it has been proven to us, when the shackles of slavery are removed from the mind and body, that freedom then knows no boundaries and mysteries will become knowledge.

The old history books and scriptures are there for us to study and learn from them as written. We are certainly made aware that those medieval rulers were not only political masters but were also meddling to command the spiritual guidance of the people. They were very convincing to be the chosen ones from the god of their time, and this extra self-glory enhanced their power and arrogance. The control was in their hands to condemn or save at will and to make war and peace to their heart's content. They were the ones who waved the so-called rod of God, killing opposing factions whether they were religious or political—justice was being served! This dictatorial ideology is still being practised today by the remnants of a few such nations still in existence. Their subjects are ready to die without a cause or question because their "god-man" promised his killers a choice place in heaven. Such contemptible beliefs have given them momentary highs throughout history and eventually destroyed the nation, but somehow those evil seeds germinated and bore the fruits of destruction.

It always amazes me to think in this religious age, why do so few heed the warning of Jesus: "Ye shall reap as ye have sown"? This saying is not hearsay but is the very law of compensation, which follows as truly as day follows night. Tragic errors in religious beliefs have devastated kingdoms throughout the ages, and the blood of the innocent flowed like rivers. Has man not been shaken to his very soul to realize that the gods of the times, which I call them, have nothing in common with the God of Love today? Christians only have to read the Old Testament of the Bible to familiarize themselves with the many slaughters in the name of their god that occurred during the life of Moses. You will read of all the cunning and deceptive planning by their god on how to attack their enemies.

Those orders were oftentimes attempts to overpower defenceless people living peacefully in their own land. According to Moses, God also gave the order to kill every woman and child and to save only the gold. Because he fulfilled those bloodthirsty actions, do we have a right to ask if we are talking about the same God who gave Moses the Ten Commandments, including, "Ye shall not kill" and "Love thy fellow man as thyself"? I am asking myself if the same God had a change of scheme and then turned around to give orders to kill women and children again and again.

My heart was yearning to ask these questions because I needed answers. Without them, Love and God would be a cruel joke. Religion has no answers to these questions; it is considered a sin to question God or the church in such matters. Now I believe that taking such a stand as not to question God about His atrocities of inhuman acts committed is wrong. How can we possibly profess to love a God whose actions we deplore, and why should He not be accountable to His devotees seeking the Truth? Whenever such difficult decisions arise, I quote again Jesus the Christ, "Seek and ye shall find"—these words are directed within. He did not say, "read and believe," because He was aware, and said so, that scriptures were full of men's laws and did not reflect the ways of God.

To me, "Seek and ye shall find" was the only way to start my search for Truth within. This way, I do not have to rely on tainted messages from other people. My perseverance was well worth the effort, and I found that God was not offended whatsoever; as a matter of fact, He is pleased with our true desire. "Ask and it shall be given." I can attest to this law as well because this means we will receive answers, which are, to us, like miracles. Anyone in this world who says that questioning God is a sin is mistaken. The message of Jesus was to seek and to ask. I did, and have had my questions answered ever since. Try it yourself; take Him by His own Word and prove it to yourself that the Spirit of God converses with us from within any time and anywhere. If you are a seeker of Truth, you shall be filled to overflowing.

Devotion, prayer, and meditation for inspirational guidance have given me the direction and understanding of God as a creative mind omnipresent in the whole of creation and in everything. It is from this glow, which touches us from time to time, that we feel peaceful, relaxed, elated or inspired, depending on the interpretation of our senses. God awareness will depend upon the inner desire of man to achieve communion of soul expression. This comes in subtle forms if we are understandingly receptive. No matter who you are, where you are or what you are, the Holy Spirit is within and we have no choice in the matter. However, I am deeply convinced, knowing and appreciating this blessing, that a pillar of strength is infused into the receptive souls. Again, ignorance of it will have the opposite effect, and such people can turn only to themselves to brood with their sensual feelings of hopelessness, frustration, and loneliness in difficult times.

God awareness through His omnipresence, which Jesus called the Holy Ghost, bathes man in spiritual sunshine. We experience similar restoration when our bodies are rejuvenated in the warmth of the sun. We should always feel close to God and, as I mentioned above, the spiritual warmth is not only a thought or a temporary feeling during the time you are in church or praying, but rather it should become a condition in your life and that without it you cannot conceive being alive. Jesus said, "I and my Father are one," and He wanted us to feel this same closeness. That is why He so often stressed, "Keep my commandments, follow me, I am the Way."

Jesus knew our worldly priorities or lustful desires and all excesses imaginable are the shackles binding mankind to a repetitious destiny of self-destruction. To break away from this habitual cycle of life,we need faith to follow in His path to a better way of life. He informed us well how difficult such a transition would be in the following verses in Matthew 7:13–14: "Enter ye in at the strait gate: for wide is the gate, and broad the way, that leadeth to destruction, and many there be which go in thereat: Because strait is the gate, and narrow is the way, which leadeth unto life, and few be there that find it."

We can clearly see He expected only a small percentage would find the way during His lifetime because Jesus was aware that most men had no connection at that time to the spiritual soul. For century upon century, man was ruled by barbarians and "force" was the logic in life, whereas Love was still unknown! Awareness was solely expressed through the perishable senses of the body, which dictate mainly on favor to please mammon, meaning you must strive for power and riches to be somebody.

Once there, nobody questions your status quo and you are received into the clone club of power by religious and political groups as an honorable member. Jesus was made aware that man must find a balance and communication between the two forces of body and soul. The inner self is forever trying to influence our sensual consciousness with the Philosophy of Love, despite our body's continual rejection.

I am extremely honored to bring into the world a formula to help mankind remain on the path in order to fulfill the glory of Love and righteousness. Only here on earth can those battles be worked out between body and soul before redemption can begin. Harmony and peace are the goals and purposes for our reincarnation on this planet so we can finally emerge from the uncertainty of darkness and deceit into the everlasting brightness of the Truth: "The Truth that shall make you whole and free."

The spiritual mixing bowl is the tool whereby any man, woman or child can fulfill the Philosophy of Love. In applying this wisdom, man would finally be in control of his duality. Because of this gift, man would not suffer again; the evilness would be snuffed out like a fire deprived of oxygen. He said, "Therefore be ye perfect like your Father is in Heaven, and sin no more."

Since the beginning of creation, the Truth of life was meant to be in totality with the expression of Love throughout the whole cycle of all living creatures. Unfortunately, on this planet, Earth, man has evolved to become an excessist, overindulging in all his ways, especially when it comes to power and riches. The kings of greed left behind legacies of destruction, sickness, famine, and endless grief and sorrow. As long as memory has served mankind, history can show us that no generation passed by without the word *war* being spoken. Heaven forbid, even the gods were portrayed as warriors who were said to be siding with their chosen people.

Such teaching and primitive thinking still prevail among many religions and people around the world today. "Remember" the God who killed the first-born of Egypt? "Remember" the God who ordered Moses to kill all women and children and save only the gold? "Remember" the God who told Moses to remove the lepers from the camp wherein he would be dwelling instead of healing them? "Remember" the God who planned the Holocaust of Jericho? "Remember" the God of Adam and Eve? Because of their sin, He cursed mankind to death for evermore. "Remember" the God of

179

Noah and the Flood, which God regretted later and then promised not to annihilate life on this earth again? What happened to this God? Was He getting old and senile, a trend occurring in man?

I could go on and on with man's make-believe gods and would like to remind the readers of this book that such beliefs did not come by free choice. People under barbarous and autocratic rulers were cursed into accepting the teachings of the land or die! Countless examples of such killings can be read in the Old Testament, and manlike traits were attributed to the gods of the times, displaying all the evil man can possibly create. Man's vision of God was likened to his own sensual character and lack of spiritual sense, or people purposefully used God to further their advantage for power and greed and to justify war and destruction. The above demonstrates the life and philosophy of the kingdoms of this world.

The teachings of Jesus Christ have definitely influenced mankind in a gradual change for the better. Brave men fought, and are still fighting, for a better form of democracy. The United States and its allies are the leading powers behind it, and because of it, Communism in Eastern Europe was derailed and has been declining ever since. This direction, we hope, will eventually eliminate barbarous dictatorships and autocracy of religion. As our educational systems improve, illiteracy will decline and the hearts of man will be demanding spiritual truth evermore. The assistance of the spiritual mixing bowl will give a new dimension to an era when the God of Love will be reigning, and man will have another chance to reach for peace and harmony in the Philosophy of Love.

23

Worldly and Spiritual Achievements

No religion or life philosophy can have a final chapter until we have attained the full understanding of the purpose of life. How, then, can arrogant wise men finalize the teachings of God when there are no limitations for the Holy Spirit? Great inventions have come and gone, and new ones are continuously improving tools to serve mankind in its endless struggle for more production and a better life. How jubilant the Stone Age inventors must have felt when they found stones to use as knives and sharp cones for spears, axes, hammers, and finally arrows. This progress of discovery probably took thousands of years. Along came the era of metal tools and jewelry of many shapes and forms; then art and culture must have reached new heights. Mankind must have marvelled anew at its inspired creative ability. Unfortunately, as with any new major invention, I believe it created new power, which, in turn, was used for the evil purpose of new tribal warfare.

Such competition continues into this day, and again we have reached fantastic heights. A hundred years of phenomenal industrial revolution has brought us into the space age, and landing on the moon was a miraculous achievement, with mankind having believed previously that this realm was only for the angels and gods. We harvest with fancy combines instead of a sickle, robots do the work of multitudes of men, and we have computers that surpass the genius of man. Have we reached the end of new discoveries?

I am told it is only the beginning of what is yet to come. It is very interesting to observe that throughout history no ruler has ever stopped such progress of science. To proclaim it as the ultimate achievement, and that no one shall add or take away from it, would be absurd because we are aware that there will never be an end to human inventions and material achievements. Scientists of today would quickly remind us, and prove, that nothing is impossible. They insist that whatever we perceive can eventually be made; we can only marvel and not deny their enthusiasm. Freedom of thinking has created the power to enable their dreams and visions to materialize, thereby supplying the world with all the material glories.

With the above description of man's sensual needs and creation, I believe I have demonstrated that the mortal man will continue to search for ever higher goals and wiser education. The limitless freedom to achieve according to each individual's desire has proven to be miraculous.

It is for the world to see that oppressed nations have not reached such a high living standard because their freedom of thinking is restricted. Free enterprise is forbidden and impaired in such places, causing individual incentives and entrepreneurial spirits to decline. Analyzing the two possibilities in our mortal life of success or poverty is directly linked to the freedom of expression in our environment. The faculties of our worldly consciousness are therefore limitless. Having examined myriad possibilities of worldly aspirations, science continues its quest to strive for ever-improved and greater goals.

What about the spiritual aspect of man? Whence have we come, and how far has man developed in his awareness of his so-called spirituality? All great religions of today originated in ancient times, and their founders and holy fathers had the power and trust to select the scriptures of old in whichever form they desired. They created beliefs and formulated dogmas to live by and teach according to their theology. In those times, I am sure, it was considered the ultimate in wisdom and truth, the whole truth and nothing but the truth. Once such doctrines were established, they were written in stone and declared infallible, never to be changed again. Religious beliefs vary greatly, but nevertheless they all proclaim to be the true and complete Word of God.

I agree with their acclaim because in my study of ancient history it clearly establishes that man believed according to the times and environmental habitat. Slavery was a way of life in which rights existed only for the king, and the choice of God was forced upon the people according to the king's command. Prophets and seers were his tools whereby he requested of them the Word of God according to their inspirational dreams and visions. From that selection, the king chose to his liking and proclaimed to his people that, "God has told me that we have to avenge!" This was the way the king was with God and God with the king.

Four hundred prophets advised the king of Israel (1 Kings 22:6–8), and it is evident that the king's inquiries of God's intentions were very rare indeed; usually they were only made when war or famine was in the wind. Opposing factions of other gods and beliefs were definitely not tolerated, which was demonstrated by Elijah who dared four hundred and fifty prophets of Baal to perform the miracle of fire (Kings 18:16–40). The prophets of Baal lost the wager and Elijah slew them all in the brook of Kishon.

I wish to recall again that Moses slew three thousand of his people when he returned from Mount Sinai with the Ten Commandments because during his absence, they wor-

183

shiped the golden calf. Somehow he found justification in committing those mass murders to appease and please his God of the times. Such atrocities are performed in some religions to this day, which proclaim the right to execute in the name of their God. Many religions were founded on ancient writings and happenings for thousands of years in the past. They believed that all those were true and continued to live in the spirit of those old warrior gods.

The revolutionary changes made by Jesus from the Old to the New Testament in the Bible definitely tell us that the teachings of old needed revisions and changes to be more in the context of Love. It was He who stressed Love as the all-important thing in life and taught, "Love thy fellow man as thyself." With this one commandment, He makes us believe that all the others are fulfilled by it. He then proclaimed that God is all Love, and if we believe Him, then we must live in the Philosophy of Love. By doing so, we fulfill the wishes of the Holy Spirit and attain the ultimate achievement for mankind. Why have we not had a Philosophy of Love to guide us throughout our lives? Is it because man has never fully understood the meaning of Love? God has been falsely identified throughout the ages as an unforgiving and punishing dictator with all the qualities of man himself.

On the assumed beginning of man, Adam and Eve were punished and banished from the Garden of Eden because they ate the apple from the Tree of Knowledge. At a later date, God is accused of flooding the world and drowning all the lives on earth, except for a chosen few. God was the warrior lord of the tribes of Israel. He called them His children and demanded, on occasion, to kill all the women and children of their enemies. He specifically ordered them to save only the gold and precious metals for the treasury of the Lord.

Another time He brought pestilence to the land of Egypt and finally killed all the first-born in the land. Having such a horrendous history, isn't there a question we must ask? Was that the same god who wrote the commandments on the stone tablets, which were given to Moses with the inscription, "Thou shalt not kill"? Is Jesus talking about the same God when He said, "God is Love"? Can we, in our hearts, really justify such terrible abomination and still proclaim love for Him? I like to believe they followed only out of jittery fear because the king demanded conformity to his belief or death.

The God of Love has never been taught by any religion because religions have always looked upon Him as being a superior man of the past, with a mixed quality of good and evil. Lack of spiritual knowledge and the gods of evil traits have darkened the soul of man, and because of it, he has suffered continuously for thousands of years. Wars, pestilence, famine, fears, and troubled minds are the harvest of the seeds sown by man throughout the ages. Changes will not occur until education and adaptation to the Philosophy of Love prevails in all nations of the world. A God of evil traits must vanish from the minds of the people in this world because of His barbaric and untrue philosophy. In such teachings of darkness, man has always found justification to do evil in return, and a vicious circle of revenge and punishment has plagued him ever since. Man must free himself of this spiritual and physical self-destruction and ready himself for the new era to come with the God of Love. The gods of the times will belong to the bygone ages of the pharaohs and the enslaved history of the Dark Ages.

Man has put much time and effort into the struggle of politics and industrial advancement to better the standard of living. We are continuously improving, and new ideas are necessary for the betterment of this world. Taking into consideration all efforts and educational advancements of the last hundred years, man has marked only the beginning of greater and nobler ideas on the horizon. In the light of this constant renewal, what gives religions the stance that spiritual utopia has been reached? Their dogmas are thousands of years old, and no new knowledge has been added. Those beliefs were originated and compiled by barbarian tribes and forced upon the people by their kings. Through a political system called dictatorship, religion has managed to keep its sheep in the corrals without a "bleat." I am foretelling that those medieval fortunes will not last.

In the new age of higher education and with the continuing contempt toward dictatorship around the world, minds everywhere will express themselves freely. The time will then come when religious dogmas will be open for discussion because Truth and Love must be found. A future congregation will demand much more than they are given today. To not question God and the Church and to follow blindly will become behaviors of the past. The Bible will become a book of history, which it rightly is. The endless stories of the Old Testament are the preachers' golden eggs, which they are plugging for all they are worth. The time will come when people will no longer be impressed by their antiques because those characters of old will be judged according to the new Philosophy of Love. Gods of wars and pestilence will withdraw into the shadows of history, and the sun will shine only for the new God of Love.

Man's spiritual reform has begun and will continue for a hundred years. This is the first time the duality of the living soul will be clearly understood. The spiritual mixing bowl will also help mankind to stay on the path, and for the first time, he will realize that destiny is of his own making. God of Love will hide no secrets from those who seek in honesty and in truth. The fruits of reward will be peace, balance, and harmony. God of Love will be the reigning glory into all four corners of the world, and opposing doctrines will turn into fading fringe organizations. Communism is on its way toward change, and so will religions, especially those using a similar ruling system.

The United Nations must continue to boycott dictatorships because it is the only force that can bring about such political changes. I pray this trend will continue, that democracy will prevail and be fine tuned. Foreign aid to Third World countries should be under much better control. Billions of dollars of such help goes straight into the bank accounts of unsavoury rulers instead of being used for the purpose it was intended. We must see to it that such aid will reach the starving people and to control the money that should go to the intended projects. We must restrain our politicians from wasting our tax dollars on unscrupulous dictatorial regimes, people must become more involved with and more demanding of political leaders, and absolute honesty and open dialogue should be a must. We can remind ourselves that misery is not created by God but by man himself. We should be especially careful to whom we entrust the leadership of our country and the United Nations. Their offices are so often abused in order to gain self-glorification and high wages for a job they are not capable of executing effectively, so it is up to us voters to prevent such abuse.

Why do politicians not have the courage to tax all religions, cults, and sects, which have businesses and large savings accounts in direct competition with the private sectors in our economy? Why should those riches not be taxed? Jesus stressed that sufficient into the day is the evil thereof; He did not believe in riches for the preaching populace. It is reasonable to have money for the upkeep of the church and its staff, but every dollar beyond that expense should be given to the hungry of the world or should be taxed like every other business in the community. This would eliminate the godly profiteers and corrupted prophets from harvesting billions from misled followers.

I also believe the time has come to correct the wicked perception and command to fear God. It was the convenient whip for the meek, and it expresses intolerance of love. To fear someone is repulsive to our soul and does not convey a gentle desire of love. Neither will it instil confidence and trust in someone we are supposed to confide in and adore. Are they praying to God out of fear, or should they pray to Him in trust and love? The latter is the only bell ringing to the God of Love, but fear is the bell for the masters of hell. Therefore, anyone believing in the God of Love should pray out of love from the heart and soul.

Fruits of Worship

The source of everything in its subtle state
Misunderstood, comprehending of the soul must wait.
It was known and taught eons before,
What does it matter what you adore?
If you love idols or saints, the stars or the sun,
It is all an expression of creation of God or the Son.
Explore His will to find the glory of Love,
Because of its fruit we cannot get enough.
The sweet savor will open heaven on earth for you,
And if you pray, the philosophy of Love will come true.

24

Man and Cosmic Laws

It is generally believed that in our time the laws of the land and that of religion are in harmony and derive from the laws of the cosmic or God. Nothing could be further from the truth because we are molding, changing, and using the planet earth very irresponsibly. Originally it was meant that all creatures, including Homo sapiens, adapt to the cycle of nature rather than nature to them. This imbalance is prevalent in the reckless pollution of our atmosphere. Short-term advantages for the sake of wealth are exploiting our substratum without any consideration of the long-term effect.

Cosmic laws and order are in the Book of Life, those inspirations are the guidelines for us to follow. They are crucial for mankind because there is no preconceived destiny as so widely perceived by religions. It is our choice to harmonize with natural and spiritual laws or to perish in willful self-destruction. Make-believe gods will not rescue anyone from such a dilemma. History has proven again and again that the innocent will suffer equally by the perpetrators breaking the laws of the universe. Ignorance of them, or arrogance, does not compensate for mistakes; only adherence to the laws and love will guide us into the favourable lifestyle here on this planet Earth.

Our use of science should be the forerunner of management and industry to assess the impact beforehand, and not only to rectify the damages already done to the environment.

We see a similar folly in our health system. If more emphasis would be put into preventive medicine, sickness and diseases would be greatly reduced. Starting with hygiene and proper foods, science could establish a guideline for healthy living, then the need for hospitals would probably be halved.

The justice system around the world is prohibitive and expensive and does not work for prevention nor for determining the appropriate punishment for crime. Prisons are becoming more elaborate and expensive, especially in the Western world. The whole system is catering to the prisoners' rights in permitting continuous appeals and by maintaining a flawed parole system at the expense of hardworking taxpayers. This spending is out of control, and no country can really afford the inefficiency demonstrated in our remand system and in the courts of this day.

The paradox called justice has determined that a life sentence should be twenty-five years. However, a string of options called paroles and appeals can reduce that sentence to fifteen years or even down to ten years. Such grace will be judged by the appropriate boards depending upon the reports of rehabilitation and good behaviour. Those routine administrations are encouraging neglect of justice throughout the system. A judge can feel immune to his verdicts because the defendant can make use of the above options. Leniency, especially for juveniles, breeds contempt. The cost to taxpayers is horrendous because by the time these juveniles are brought before the courts and then sent home without even a slap, they have learned there is nothing to lose in repeating another offense. The law cannot charge youngsters under the age of ten years, which means they are free to assault or commit any crime they please, especially against younger children. I staunchly believe that if the strap was administered during the custody of all those young criminals before they were released, it would cure 80 percent of them during the first time around.

To deter criminals of any kind, punishment must be fitting the crime committed, regardless of age. Ignorance or age does not excuse wickedness or disobedience, which must be discouraged at an early and impressionable age. The present Young Offenders Act encourages repeat offenses because of the present leniency and secrecy of young criminals. A criminal act of taking the life of another person is no less traumatic, whatever the age of the offender. We have no equal justice in our court system for a life taken except capital punishment because we do not have, as of yet, the knowledge of rehabilitation for lustful and premeditated murders.

Human emotions to forgive instead of scorn are too often applied because of the false perception of love. Realistically, the only person deserving sympathy is the bewitched and innocent victim. They are often ignored or re-abused by questions and investigations irrelevant to the crime. They are the ones in need of immediate attention and compassion because they have lived the horror of being robbed, tortured, raped, and many are often killed. All victims should be given the opportunity to express the fairness of punishment meted out by the courts to their assailants and notified upon the prisoners' release. A total change must occur if we, as a society, would like to live with less crime.

First, it must be understood that there is no criminal tolerance level acceptable. Second, all expenses accrued due to crime must be paid for by the criminals and not by the taxpayers. Third, all crime has to have a price tag, and this could easily be established in this age of computer skill. In between, variations of criminal acts can readily be adjusted as needed. Unfair and expensive judging could be greatly reduced in most criminal cases and felony charges would have a price tag where a fine should be levied whenever possible. Monetary punishments must be of equal effect for the rich and the poor alike.

For example, a traffic violation could be a half percent of the accused's net income, which the courts can establish by computer. The percentage will increase for repeat offenders so that eventually no one could afford to break the laws of the land. Prisons should have work camps for dangerous offenders to pay for their keep and crime. Other prisoners will continue working in their private jobs during the day but would have to spend their nights in jail until upkeep and crime is paid in full. No criminal will have a free ride with lawyers' fees and—regardless of age or gender—the punishment will be determined by the crime. The justice system will encompass everything that has to do with enforcing the laws, including the police force. The unemployed and young offenders will work in labour camps until restitution and justice have been served.

Capital punishment has always created the biggest controversy in our present-day criminality. Because of religion we are told that this punishment of taking the life of another is inhuman, but at the same time, we are ignoring the fact that the murderer did exactly that—an inhuman act. Religion has not explained to us what constitutes a human being. We are taking it for granted that this designation refers to all creatures called Homo sapiens. We are told that God created us in His own likeness and therefore are considered godly entities. This is a universal misunderstanding and can be proven to be untrue.

Yes, man is born a duality of body and soul or, if you please, of the flesh and the spirit. If the latter is dormant in people, Jesus called them the living dead because they have eyes but do not see, have ears but do not hear, and have a mind that does not comprehend. He was referring to spiritual inspiration and understanding, and all of His parables and doctrine were meant in this manner. This spiritual choice of each individual determines whether or not we are human beings.

The words "human being" originated not for wanting to replace mankind or Homo sapiens but to portray a characteristic of our species. The dictionary describes those specific qualities as humane, compassionate, sympathetic, and considerate toward all life and those qualities are comprised into the human code of Love, which establishes the morality standard of a people. Love is the inspiration of the "spiritual soul" and does not revert to criminality. Criminals, therefore, are only guided by the instinct of our five senses. Those alone do not make us a human being, only a creature of creation.

A murderer has forsaken the human code for his lifetime, and no living man has the right nor the justice to forgive a homicidium. We cannot give justice to such a crime but can only safeguard our society by capital punishment, excluding accidental and self-defense or in other circumstances where evidence is not conclusive. A reformed court system will be able to convey justice in our society and relieve the burden of the innocent. Until a human status or code is recognized, a decree of fairness will not serve the human race.

Love must rule our lives to overcome the evil influence of the flesh. Such behavior is termed human. If this code of Love is broken and we resort to murder, then we have abandoned the soul and our reactions are of the flesh and our thinking solely of the instinct. In this situation we have absolutely no likeness to God, having transformed ourselves into creatures of creation rather than living souls under the guidance of the Holy Spirit. To call ourselves human beings, we must demonstrate the qualities that come with the term. I call this the human code of Love.

I hope that I have successfully demonstrated above that the murderer is not a human being, and if capital punishment is warranted, he should be humanely euthanized by a veterinarian. Our present system lets some murderers go free after ten years or less for good behavior. How about the innocent victims? Do they have a second chance for good behavior? We are talking about justice. Is the life of a murderous creature more precious than that of an unfortunate human being? Those who proclaim human rights must not extend those to a merciless killer who denied all rights, even life, to his victim. Compare the instinct of a wild tiger; he will kill you at his first opportunity, whereas a tamed one will not overstep the code of Love to harm you. Are we saying that a murderer with less morality than a wild animal is a human being?

Spiritual Love creates a high morality standard and has nothing to do with sentiment or hypocrisy, nor foolishness in forgiving before restitution has taken place. For example, if we fail to correct a young child for misbehavior, he or she will ultimately grow up with criminal tendencies. If we think forgiving is godly when punishment is due, we are mistaken and sending the wrong message. Leniency will often double the burden for the innocent victim in a repeat crime because the sentence was not a deterrent the first time. "Ye shall reap as ye have sown" is the eternal law of the universe, and we are judged and punished by it into all eternity. This law should also apply to our courts if we as a society desire to lessen our out-of-control crime rate.

Those bleeding hearts who are against capital punishment are only pretenders of Love because they cannot hear the agonizing cries of the victims. Sentiment for the criminal will not correct our statistics, but proper deterrents will slow our rising crime rate down. We cannot afford the cost nor the misery criminals cause and we must be serious about fighting crime. The province of Alberta was serious about fighting rats, and it boasts to be free of that useless pest. Animal lovers might say it is not fair to exterminate such a creature just because it only takes and has absolutely nothing to give. The point here is that Alberta would not tolerate that creature and was serious about exterminating it at all costs. That is exactly how we should feel if we are serious in fighting to reduce crime.

Most criminals have made no contribution to society, but their plan is to take only the goods of others, no matter what hardship and pain they cause! Their feelings are only for themselves, and they have no Love to give; they only cause sorrow and even death on their selfish trail of destruction and crime. Are we telling them that it is okay and that we condone their lifestyle because we have been brainwashed to think that they are human beings? We must encourage the same determination of Alberta to fight criminality to extinction.

Capital punishment by injection is not "an eye for an eye," as some people choose to believe. It falls way short of equal justice because of the agonizing trauma and torture so many of the victims had to endure, which is far worse than death itself. Even though capital punishment does not compensate the crime, at least it will assure society that such a beast cannot repeat its offence. Presently, a young murderer with good behavior will be out on the streets in a few years, enabling him to repeat the crime a second time while still under the Young Offender's Act.

Most adults are released on parole in ten years or less amongst our unwary society. These criminals believe that they have paid for their deeds while they enjoyed good food, television, sports, and education at the taxpayers' expense. They also enjoy human rights to excess, which encourages them to riot and once more have their own way. Our justice system has failed us because it is set up to make the professionals rich, but it leaves the criminal unscathed financially and morally. Human rights must be forfeited until all restitution has been met for every crime. This degradation is essential if we are serious in fighting to eliminate crime.

Crime must pay its own way in the justice system, and there is no way that innocent human beings should be footing the bills for those who have forsaken the human code. Organized criminals must not be tolerated, and all businesses and properties acquired by them should automatically be confiscated and sold to support the judicial system. With these methods we can guarantee the citizens safety and a peaceful lifestyle for a society living in the Philosophy of Love. The present criminal system is totally the burden of the innocent taxpayers, including its endless appeal process, the costly parole procedure, and finally halfway houses and supervision. The above practises are a lucrative money machine for thousands of professionals across the land, mostly paid for with tax dollars.

The above burdens could all be eliminated by a more simplified computerized court system, which emphasizes and focuses on the criminals' activity. Sidetracking and confusing trials with so-called technicalities and incriminating circumstances that are unrelated to the crime, would not be admissible. All true evidence of a crime should be admissible, no matter how it was obtained. All justice is focused on the trial alone.

Therefore, on a murder charge, three judges should be presiding, plus a jury, and for dangerous offenders and criminal charges, two judges should be present and only one for lesser crimes. All the justice effort is put into this one trial, and if the offender is found guilty without any doubt, there will be no more appeals. If capital punishment is deserved, the offender will be executed on the tenth day thereafter. The present system is holding murderers on death row for years.

Some people believe in rehabilitation, but there is no trick or wisdom among the wise men proclaiming such a gift!

196

Any sentence executed in the courts must be served for the full term because there will be no parole system and no other gimmicks such as halfway houses. As I mentioned previously, every criminal will be working eight hours a day and will spend only the nights in jail, except the dangerous offenders, who must work in prison camps. Prisons should be inspected monthly for food, hygiene, tolerance, and behavior from both sides. Humane treatment is an order, but prisoners will not receive human rights to protest, nor can they make any demands. During incarceration, voting privileges will be revoked until the crime is compensated and they are released from prison amongst the society of human beings.

Good farmers have learned from their forefathers and from experience that the cosmic principle, "Ye shall reap as ye have sown" follows true as day follows night. Their wisdom to plant only the best of seeds and work the land with sweat and love, will pay off handsomely at harvest time. The same holds true of each individual, because what we are thinking today will be the seeds of tomorrow. Likewise, what religion is teaching us is supposed to be the seed of spirituality. This cosmic principle, "To reap as we have sown," will always come to pass. It is paramount in all businesses and very important in politics to lead a country into prosperity.

It is a law with a just outcome and therefore should be used by our court system as I have mentioned above. Criminality is on the rise and is out of control; therefore, foolish sentiment and leniency are messages of weakness and condonement. It is pressed upon me that criminal acts must be met with a punishment deserving of the crime. The message of nontoleration of such acts must be felt by an effective deterrent. Let us get our acts together to make our homes and streets safe again for all of us throughout the land in applying cosmic laws and justice.

25

Love to Reign

People of a democratic and free country have no more excuses to honor the traditions of barbarians. We must throw off the shackles of the Dark Ages and begin to recognize Love as a way of life. The historic gods, who surpassed the evils of man, make us wonder if it is unfair to compare those contemptible actions of their hellish era. Is it not common among pirates, as well, to love each other and share their bounty, but to have no respect and mercy upon whom they prey?

Man possesses the instrument to measure and weigh the most subtle feelings within himself, and to sort out what is good for him and what leans toward evil. Let me provide the key given to me through inspiration, which I call the spiritual mixing bowl. This guided me along the trail and through the maze of the religious jungle of man for many years. There was one who proclaimed that in Love all commandments are fulfilled. He taught and lived accordingly and was crucified because of it. He was, and continues to be, a shining star. However, His teachings have been marred by glorifying the messenger instead of the message He lived for. Jesus pointed toward the goal for us to reach and to teach, only to be hindered again and overshadowed by old-time traditions and misunderstandings of His doctrine. Spiritually, not much has been achieved by Christian religion, and until people live, preach, and practice the Philosophy of Love, they will not see the light of the true Creator, the God of Love.

All the holified Scriptures of every religion of this world, traditions, dogmas, theology, spirituality, holy places, pyramids, great temples and churches of every kind, including the prophets and the gods of the times, can be easily described as mere specks of creation; some made by the fancy of man and others by the divine spirit. It is the process of the living soul to learn and experience, to seek and to find, to seed and to harvest the lessons learned from the above creations.

Love has been treated shabbily by man. It has been used as a mere tool of pretence by the affluent of society, especially by the rulers, religious leaders, and politicians. By its use they gained the support of the masses and won their trust. This game of falsehood has been inborn in man for thousands of years. History tells us that kings and rulers were able to achieve quicker control over their subjects by force of might rather than by Love. Love was spoken but not practiced; even the gods of the times demanded Love by threats of destruction and pestilence. Love is the most abused and mistreated word in our dictionary. Now this negligent abuse of Love has been directed toward nature. This assault will backfire by choking us in our own pollution.

Love is not only for us and our families, but it must extend into business, politics, and into all worldly affairs. By the application of Love, the industrial progress will be much slower and profits somewhat smaller, but the great benefits would include clean air, good water, and fertile land. Many sicknesses will vanish and also smoking, drugs, and excesses of every kind, which are not born of Love and are harmful to the human race would disappear. Is there a chance for such a philosophy to make a beginning? Yes, mankind can either choose or reject this advocated lifestyle. The Philosophy of Love should be taught from kindergarten right through to university, in business, and in politics. It must be the number-one subject on everyone's mind. Love, through the spiritual mixing bowl, is a simple technique to live by.

The second choice is for us to continue the process of the past: suffering, pollution, sickness, famines, inequality, hate, and more wars. We are to blame, and are certainly responsible for our own actions and to whatever extreme. Nothing will change the curse of destruction unless we do it ourselves through the spiritual mixing bowl. We must live by it because harmony and the glory of God depend upon its use.

The question remains, are we going to learn from past experiences and begin to recognize that our present worldly existence is built on greed and falsehood? Truth and Love must be found through our free will. This is the only way we can face and master problems that confront us. This gift I call the spiritual mixing bowl allows us to mix the right potion of Love into the process of thought to create harmony for all decisions made by us. With the continuous use of it, we will stay on the path of the Holy Spirit and in the Philosophy of Love.

Love is pleasing and in accord with all universal laws; it is the fundamental force necessary for all life, and by its actions, the soul will be brightened. Our worldly spirit will therefore be influenced in the light of goodness, and our endeavors will bear the seeds of honor and trust. Love is the grace of the Holy Spirit, and we must be awakened to this realization that Love is the sublime philosophy of life.

Love must become the power to reign because this great universal force called love is a divine flow, the essence of life. The only reason we are not totally incensed and influenced by its vibration is because of our neglect of self. The great barrier of separation is the dictatorial force of the worldly spirit between our body and soul. The body-consciousness is the ruler of the flesh on our daily life, and it dictates our senses and our physical attributes twenty-four hours to its limits. A continuous struggle for the survival and pleasures of the body has always been its primary importance.

Man, therefore, may pass through life without any awareness of his own soul. Because of this dormancy of the soul, not even a rich man can find the joy of inner tranquillity that our soul has to offer. This spiritual breath of life is the medium between the conscious living man and the God of Love. I want to be very specific when I talk about God. I always refer to the God of Love of all creation, and I certainly do not want this Supreme Being confused with all the man-made imposters of the times. Let me explain what I mean by that expression. We have had religion for thousands of years, and all throughout history, we find that man idolized gods of all imaginations. Once those images were accepted in man's mind, he sanctified them and they became most powerful in influencing his way of life. Countless generations of descendants believed in those glorified imposters and to this very day have worshiped those gods of the times.

There were always those with inspirational guidance of a spiritual nature, and they tried to influence and reshape the word of the god of their time. However, prophetic messages available to the king were not always selected according to the spiritual need of the people and country. They had to fit the mood and desire of the ruler, oftentimes creating contradiction between the kings and the prophets. Such unfavorable messages could provoke the killings of the prophets.

Religion adopted a similar regime. It happened to Jesus when He was killed because they did not like His way and His message. Many of us wonder if Jesus would be recognized by the churches should He appear amongst us today. I do not believe so because of their general attitudes in declaring their ways perfect and infallible. Such a stance distorts and defies humbleness and the true teachings of Jesus. He died for the Philosophy of Love, but Christians have failed to follow His teachings and to live accordingly.

People are still dying of hunger, and the world continues to be in distress. Religion failed miserably in helping these unfortunates spiritually and financially. We cannot stop progress in any manner because it is against the cosmic laws, and if we do advance, it must be in recognition of the law of compensation. I maintain that pollution must also be of religious concern because it is a silent killer of man and beast. It destroys and poisons the flower garden of creation. Are not the churches standing in the middle of this garden, doing nothing to alleviate this universal cancer?

The gods of the times were credited with good and evil deeds. They blessed and they cursed, they saved and killed, and they loved some and hated others. Those contradictions, I am told, were created in the mind of man and his worldly spirit. Misunderstandings, misinterpretations, willful denials, blind acceptance, greed, power, and riches are all to blame for the glorification of the counterfeit creators because you cannot say God is Love if He has traits of revenge and anger, jealousy and hate.

In our time of education, great multitudes are beginning to understand the fallacy behind such teachings. Many true seekers will begin searching within their souls to find the path to the "God of Love." The time is near when man's conscience will be craving for more knowledge of this true God. Just being content to belong to a flock of sheep going in circles with no spiritual destiny will no longer be satisfying. Brainwashing has only worked because of man's unawareness of the Holy Spirit.

The spiritual mixing bowl is the threshold and the new beginning for the Philosophy of Love. It is the source of enlightenment for the living soul because from it we derive the perception and inspiration of all goodness and justice prevailing over the divine guidance for our life. Along the way man has evolved mentally and spiritually according to his experiences and educational availability. During the last one hundred years of industrial revolution, it certainly opened the eyes of millions of people who then began to realize another way of life.

Equality, freedom of expression, and so on, have given us a political system called democracy. Because of it, slavery and dictatorship have been reduced throughout the world. This new trend has also brought attention to the environmental concerns across our planet. Those problems cannot be resolved without the total cooperation of all the countries of the world. It is apparent that the intelligence of man has a long way to go before we can envision a peaceful and harmonious life on our planet earth.

Technologically, man's inspirations and achievements have reached the sky, and within the coming decades, we cannot fathom his future aspirations. Hopefully, I believe it will be on the constructive side and only for peaceful purposes. Taking into consideration the spiritual advancement of man, we must ask, "How far have we come?" Looking back over the past few thousand years, we have a legacy of many great religions with billions of followers. All teachings and dogmas have their origin in ancient writings or scrolls, tablets of stones, and cones produced by prophets, seers, and the kings.

Our present-day Bible is compiled from early Hebrew writings, dating back to Abraham. His first son, Ismael, born to Heather, is the beginning of the religion Islam, and Abraham's second son, Isaac, born to his first wife, Sarah, resulted in the beginning of the Hebrew religion. The New Testament is the teaching of Jesus, and according to the Bible, his family tree traced back to Isaac and Abraham, making Christianity the third belief from the patriarch Abraham.

The Bible has given us the insight into how these people lived during those historic times, especially from the regions of the Middle East and Arabia. Christianity is by far the largest religion today, with a following of close to a billion people. It has splintered into hundreds of different organizations, cults, and creeds, each one proclaiming the ultimate utopia of belief. In my search for the God of Love, I have found all of their dogmas written in stone, never to be questioned! It seems such folly that spiritual limits in religious dogmas have been set. Such religious finality has given the end for knowledge rather than the great beginning because spiritual wisdom has no limitations. A religion proclaiming to possess all spiritual knowledge has reached the degree of stagnation that Jesus called the spiritual darkness. He said that they have eyes but cannot see, they have ears and do not hear, therefore their minds are closed and they fail to understand.

If religion wants to teach God of Love, it will have to know the Philosophy of Love because nothing else is of such importance as to lay the foundation for the spirit of Truth. Jesus promised that He would pray to His Father for you in order to receive a Comforter, to enlighten you of all Truth, and that the Holy Ghost shall be with you eternally. Continuity of His doctrine is important, not by twisted words or mere repetitions, but by His spiritual inspirations. "Seek and ye shall find" are words of encouragement and a promise to every living soul. It is worthwhile for the human race to abide by the cosmic laws in order to find peace and joy in the Philosophy of Love.

Sunlight—Godlight Equals: Love

"Sunlight" is the life-giving force our bodily functions depend upon. Its warmth radiates all the comfort and joy throughout our bodies and minds; it also brings the necessary tranquillity for good health and continuity to the living soul. It is no longer a mystery to today's educated men that without this great blessing of the sun, all of life's food chain would vanish into oblivion, and with it all life on earth. The sun is the great wheel, which continuously turns nature into our favour.

EQUALLY,

"Godlight" shines through our soul, performing likewise, but in the spiritual capacity upon the living soul. Our soul is continuously charged with this divine flow, and consciously we should be aware of the great blessing of this dual function in us. Because of this pulsing interaction, the living soul will express this perfect combination of both lights as Love.

26

Here and Now

Have you ever sat down and seriously contemplated your own self and asked, "What do I want to achieve? Is my life satisfactory so far, or disappointing?" What about sickness and health and your future? What about love for yourself and others, your mother, father, sisters, brothers and all relatives? Could you improve on all other relationships? Are you generous or selfish?

Doing this, you will find yourself quite mysterious. Such analysis should be done more often, by adults and children alike; it will enhance self-esteem. You may also realize that your presence in this world is important to others. Because of our hectic lifestyles, the study of self is totally neglected by most of us, with the mistaken assumption that we know everything about ourselves. Self-criticism or self-praise may have been overdue to turn the wheel of life at the right speed for the morrow. After all, those are the main concerns in our sensual world, to please the desires of the body. We do wonder if there is more to life, or if this is our sole purpose of existence.

Through my own tests of self-study, I found my consciousness not only satisfied my worldly needs but also started a gradual awakening from within. Maybe we feel a longing to be more righteous or understanding in business and to our fellowman. Millions of you out there, I am sure, have had an experience at one time or another in which you had the impulsive urge to check on your children or spouse, look into a certain place, or do something unforeseen. Lo and behold, your action saved a life or you found something you treasured that had slipped your memory for so long and finally it is yours again. Maybe you had a warning impulse and avoided a disaster. Where did these hunches come from, so precise at the crucial moment? It makes one wonder.

Most were accounted for as a stroke of luck, yet others will call them a miracle. There was a time in my life when either assumption was good enough for me and I thought, *Who cares?* Many decades later I do care about where those premonitions came from. Through prayer, meditation, and constant searching within, I can proclaim with an inspired conscience, and with trumpets blowing, that there is more to *Homo sapiens* than just a body and the five senses with a brain. I actually became aware that man possesses a spiritual soul, including a computerlike library of stored experiences since creation. I am well aware that many Christians have a different interpretation—they believe that the body and flesh is all there is of man and that they term it the living soul, which turns into dust until the day of resurrection.

"Let the dead bury the dead," Jesus said, because He even rebuked His own disciples many times for not comprehending the spiritual meanings of His parables and teachings. "Man must be born of water and of the spirit," He said, and made sure that we understood our spiritual heritage, which must be awakened in order to function as intended by God.

On the other hand, worldly excesses are demanded according to the desires of the flesh. It is written that God made man out of the dust from the earth and bestowed through His nostrils the breath of life, which He called a living soul. The breath of life and the spiritual soul is the same thing, and an individualized entity from the essence of the

Creator. Since man shall not live on bread alone, spiritual food for the soul is equally important. Yes, I too read the Bible, not only once but a few times over. It is rich in history for man to learn by those experiences in order to avoid similar disasters of his making and to select cosmic laws and principles for the betterment of mankind.

There are also many other inspired writings throughout the world, which have given man new religions for a better way of life because of them. All these writings will proclaim to be the only Truth of this world, even though the interpretations many times contradict themselves. Because of this confusion, I forward my important questions to the Holy Spirit for clarification. No doctrine, teachings or book has my acceptance of Truth until the answers are received from within my soul, which is the divine channel between God and man.

Once a well-known minister expressed his view about the Holy Bible. "Without it," he said, "we would have nothing to believe in." This, to me, is a tragedy of a forlorn soul, and I must ask, "Has such a man understood the message of Christ and yet never communicated directly with God?" How shallow can faith be? Spiritual Truth must be experienced between God and man; until then all doctrines are uncertain assumptions in flattery of the false prophets.

The Will of God taught by Jesus is the vitality of the living soul so that life can be experienced in the Philosophy of Love. This bestows upon a human being the blessings and light required to inspire men to a higher morality standard. There is absolutely no other way for mankind to achieve the desired harmony and peace. No spiritual messengers, prophets, or Sons of God, including Jesus, can do more than show us the way, but the fruits thereof will have to be borne through our actions. This is the law pertaining to our free will.

Men's Strife

Pride marches on in this devious age,
Always to be hampered by demons.
Emperors and conquerors built always a cage
To suppress the conquered for aeons.
Scientists worked day and night to make the balloon,
And with great pay glorious achievements are swift.
We have evidence, tomorrow they will be on the moon,
Marvellous achievement, if nothing is left adrift?
What else could be of such interest
In our life, but work hard to be a rich man's clone?
I have to ask again about demons, their power and zest?
What about our forgotten soul, how far have we gone?

A disciple said unto Jesus, "Lord, suffer me first to go and bury my father." But Jesus said unto him, "Follow me; and let the dead bury the dead." *Dead* was the word He used for those with a forgotten soul, and He also said, "That which is born of the flesh is your body; and that which is born of the spirit is your soul. Marvel that I said unto thee, ye must be born again."

Therefore I extend to you the spiritual mixing bowl, and by its application, you will awaken and bring about the resurrection of your spiritual Soul. This will enable us to partake again in the life intended by the Will of God in the Philosophy of Love.

27

Spiritual Dimensions

The great cosmos seems endless to our comprehension. Our galaxy with the sun, moon, and twinkling stars are the best understood because they continually influence life on earth. All the elements that influenced man since his first breath have never ceased to be, and we can only marvel at the complexity of life itself. In general, everything is taken for granted until one day our health begins to fail, drought and famine strike, or we lose our forests and homes through fire and floods. The elements of nature have their own spiritual dimensions just like all things created in the universe. It is surrounded and filled with its own spirit; we sense but cannot see such spirit.

The meaning behind the word *spiritual,* I believe, is grossly misunderstood, even by orthodox religion. Man himself is multispiritual, brought about by his duality of body and soul. By birth he is influenced by the worldly spirit and also inspired by the soul consciousness of the Holy Spirit. This divine presence, if acknowledged, gives man the capability to master destiny in complete harmony with our planet. It was meant to be this way. But instead man's overwhelming influence by the worldly spirit, which is of his own choosing, relished power and greed as the aim of his accomplishments. Gods and dogmas were fashioned to suit the ruling of the elite. For them the task of controlling the ever-increasing population became more and more difficult as the centuries passed.

Jesus was among the first to influence man with His inspired teachings of love given to Him by the Holy Spirit. In those days religions were not about to change their dogmas, which were written in stone. Regardless of how sound His teachings were, only a few would listen to His words; the miracles He performed drew the crowds and seemed to have imparted a lasting impression. Would the Second Coming of Jesus be any different today from the first time? I do not believe so, because the dogmas of today are still written in stone, and Jesus would preach the same message again, namely the "Philosophy of Love." The Holy Spirit does not change its manner; it is written in Luke 9:55: "But he turned, and rebuked them, and said, Ye know not what manner of spirit ye are of."

Jesus is mentioning the manner of the spirit because he knew the difference between the worldly spirit and the Holy Spirit. I believe that His teachings would be seen as revolutionary today as they were at that time and that His kingdom of the spirit has not changed either. I can tell you of the disappointment He would face because He would find mammon instead of the Philosophy of Love. When children are dying of hunger, He would not praise us. He would ask us, "Where are my commandments and why do you not fulfill them?" Autocratic churches of today would not know Him because they glorify Jesus the man, His showmanship, His personality, and the miracles He performed. Would He do the same things again? Jesus was not occupied with His person. He was only concerned with His teachings, the Word of God, and the laws given to Him. Those were the only things Jesus glorified and was committed to these being His spiritual life.

Good and evil are the two spirits we are talking about,

and because of his duality, man is influenced by both. It has been argued which is more important, "To accept Jesus into your heart or to do His Will?" To me it is one and the same because I see no difference in the choice. You cannot have one without the other and still call yourself a Christian. Whenever Jesus healed the sick, He told them, "Go and sin no more." In Saint John 15:10, He says, "If ye keep my commandments, ye shall abide in my love, even as I have kept my Father's commandments and abide in His love."

Man has to reform his worldly spirit, and the New Age method of doing that is the continued use of the spiritual mixing bowl. Your ideas will be washed clean of possible evil influences in your family, business, and political affairs. In this philosophy it does not matter how rich or poor you are because each person is of equal importance in bringing about the lifestyle of Love into this world. Wars will be eliminated, there will be no more cheating and cruelty, and the rightful equality between all races and sexes will be attained. Evilness is a spirit created solely in man's mind and can only be compensated in this sensual world by eliminating evil in our present cycle of life.

There is not, and never was, another way to salvation. The mixing bowl is our way to redemption and to remind us that the Spirit of Jesus is expressed in His Word and not in His body. Saint John 15:12 states, "This is my commandment, that ye love one another, as I have loved you."

Spiritual harmony between body and soul was the aim of Jesus's teachings. Regardless of our religious affiliations, love should always be supreme. It was the goal of Jesus to bring into this world the knowledge of how to live in peace. The understanding of Love is a requirement in order to have the truth revealed from within. The churches are full of songs and praises for the redeemers who walked the earth. They were the renowned prophets like Jesus, who taught that redemption is at hand because of their messages. Unless we understand and accept them and live accordingly, they are not, and cannot be, our redeemers until we are enlightened through their doctrines.

Redemption, of course, is necessary for both the body and soul in order to balance the influence of both spirits, and a middle ground has to be found, which is harmony. That is the reason why we are made aware of the spiritual mixing bowl. It will cleanse our thinking and will give us the wisdom to work diligently in harmony and justice in the "Philosophy of Love."

It was said by Jesus that a rich man will find it hard to get into the kingdom of heaven, but the question arises, "Were those riches achieved solely by greed and power?" It is evident that few have reached the pinnacle of great wealth with love, but in our society, unsavoury behaviour is commonplace to reach those goals. The weaknesses in our educational system must be overcome by continued use of the spiritual mixing bowl.

Philosophy of Love is the inauguration for the next one hundred years of a long overdue spiritual reform. It will mark the discovery of inspirational knowledge, which has never been experienced before for millions of followers. The world will be blessed with insight of great spiritual significance because the freedom of mind and soul has no boundaries in communion with the Holy Spirit. Love must reign over our actions, and destiny will be blessed with harmony.

Masses of people will resurrect their souls, brought about by the use of the spiritual mixing bowl. Because of this new lifestyle, millions will pray to the Holy Spirit and will be blessed in living the Philosophy of Love. The Holy Spirit is to our soul what the fresh air is to our lungs and is available at all times. I stress, do not pollute those two principal

213

elements because without them there would be no heaven or earth.

It will open to us a new way whereby we can overthrow the shackles of evil and be reborn with gentler ways, with more compassion and yearning to pursue all virtues of love. As a family, in business or in politics, a desire will stir to work for the common good of all people. A rich man is a blessing to everyone who needs a job, and a poor man is important to fulfill that job. If both live under the Philosophy of Love, then every person is important and respected in a society in which the Philosophy of Love is the constitution of the country.

Epilogue

Crowning

In hope that the temporal can envision the eternal by the way of the mixing bowl and enlighten the human race to the Will of God. The Philosophy of Love is the order in the Book of Life, and its kindness will restore justice and render salvation. Our actions will shine in the spirit of Love, the shackles of the Lucifers will vanish, and evil will no longer be condoned. Hell on earth must be erased to bring about the heavenly affiliation with the God of Love. In Him we will find the resurrection of our soul, the virtues of Love, Salvation, Justice, and Truth, and finally the world shall be blessed with harmony and peace.

Bibliography

Bible, King James Version. London: Eyre and Spottiswood, Coronation, 1953.

Cayce, Edgar. *You Can Remember Your Past Lives.* New York: Warner, 1989.

Daniken, E.V. *The Gold of the Gods.* New York: Putnam's, 1974.

Encyclopaedia Britannica.

Lewis, Spencer H. *The Mystical Life of Jesus.* San Jose, California: Rosicrucian Press, 1953.

Living Bible, paraphrased. Wheaton, Illinois: Tyndale House, 1971.

Origen. Mahwah, New Jersey: Paulist Press, 1979.

The World and Its Peoples. New York: Greystone, 1964.

Index

Bible Quotations